ORTHO'S All About

Lawns

Meredith₀ Books
Des Moines, Iowa

Ortho® Books
An imprint of Meredith® Books

All About Lawns
Principal Garden Writer: Warren Schultz
Editor: Marilyn Rogers
Contributing Editor: Leona H. Openshaw
Contributing Technical Editors: Roch Gaussoin,
    Ali Harivandi
Art Director: Tom Wegner
Copy Chief: Catherine Hamrick
Copy and Production Editor: Terri Fredrickson
Contributing Copy Editors: Martin Miller, Ed Malles,
    Carol Boker, Diane Witosky
Contributing Proofreaders: Kathy Roth Eastman,
    Steve Hallam, Mary Pas
Contributing Illustrator: Jonathan Clark, Wayne Clark
Contributing Prop/Photo Stylists: Mary E. Klingamon,
    Diane Munkel
Indexer: Don Glassman
Electronic Production Coordinator: Paula Forest
Editorial and Design Assistants: Kathleen Stevens,
    Karen Schirm
Production Director: Douglas M. Johnston
Production Manager: Pam Kvitne
Assistant Prepress Manager: Marjorie J. Schenkelberg

Additional Editorial Contributions from
Art Rep Services
Director: Chip Nadeau
Designer: lk Design

Meredith® Books
Editor in Chief: James D. Blume
Design Director: Matt Strelecki
Managing Editor: Gregory H. Kayko
Executive Ortho Editor: Benjamin W. Allen

Director, Sales & Marketing, Retail: Michael A. Peterson
Director, Sales & Marketing, Special Markets:
    Rita McMullen
Director, Sales & Marketing, Home & Garden Center
    Channel: Ray Wolf
Director, Operations: George A. Susral

Vice President, General Manager: Jamie L. Martin

Meredith Publishing Group
President, Publishing Group: Christopher M. Little
Vice President, Consumer Marketing & Development:
    Hal Oringer

Meredith Corporation
Chairman and Chief Executive Officer: William T. Kerr
Chairman of the Executive Committee: E.T. Meredith III

All of us at Ortho® Books are dedicated to providing you
with the information and ideas you need to enhance your
home and garden. We welcome your comments and
suggestions about this book. Write to us at:
    Meredith Corporation
    Ortho Books
    1716 Locust St.
    Des Moines, IA 50309–3023

If you would like more information on other Ortho
products, call 800-225-2883 or visit us at www.ortho.com

Thanks to
Janet Anderson, Laura Davenport, Lori Gould,
Ann Heimstra, Colleen Johnson, Aimee Reiman,
Mary Irene Swartz; Wright Tree Care, Clive, Iowa

Photographers
(Photographers credited may retain copyright ©
    to the listed photographs.)
L= Left, R= Right, C= Center, B= Bottom, T= Top
William D. Adams: p. 31 (B), 73 (T, C), 75 (C), 84 (B),
    86 (T), 87 (C);
F. P. Baxendale: p. 29 (B)
Michael Bourque/VALAN PHOTOS: p. 73 (B)
Philip Busey: p. 23 (C), 65 (B);
R. S. Byther: p. 87 (T, B), 88 (T), 89 (C);
Nick E. Christians: p. 74 (inset);
Thomas W. Cook: p. 30 (B);
Crandall & Crandall: p. 21 (T), 52 (T), 89 (T);
R. Todd Davis: p. 14 (T);
Alan & Linda Detrick: p. 50 (R), 71 (T);
Jim F. Dill: p. 66 (TL), 78 (B), 82 (BL), 83 (C), 86 (C);
Derek Fell: p. 9 (BL);
Charles Marden Fitch: p. 70 (B);
John Glover: p. 34 (TR), 43 (C), 72 (C);
Chris L. Gotman/VALAN PHOTOS: p. 66 (CR);
Jerry Howard/Positive Images: p. 9 (T), 62 (T), 65 (C);
Bill Johnson: p. 70 (T);
judywhite/New Leaf Images: p. 9 (BR), 65 (T);
J. A. Kalisch: p. 78 (C); 80 (B);
Larry Kassell: p. 4 (T), 11, 16 (R), 17, 44 (T), 50 (L);
Dwight R. Kuhn: p. 10 (BL), 83 (T, B);
Michael Landis: p. 12 (inset);
Scott Leonhart/Positive Images: p. 80 (C);
Charles Mann: p. 19 (TL, TR);
Stuart McCall: p. 26 (C), 56;
Bryan McCay: p. 28, 29 (T), 48 (TR, CR), 53 (L), 54, 55,
    58, 60, 62 (B), 63 (T, B);
Eric Miltner: p. 34 (BR);
Robert & Linda Mitchell: p. 80 (T, inset), 82 (T);
Philip L. Nixon: p. 76 (L), 77, 78 (T), 81 (T), 82 (C);
Maggie Oster: p. 50 (C), 52 (inset, B);
Jerry Pavia: p. 4 (B);
Pam Peirce: p. 12 (T), 68 (C&B), 69 (T&C), 70 (C),
    71 (B), 75 (B), 88 (B);
Susan A. Roth: p. 16 (L), 19 (B), 24, 30 (C), 31 (T), 39,
    53 (R);
Larry A. Sagers: p. 9 (C), 10 (BR), 12 (B), 30 (T), 66 (TR),
    68 (T), 74 (B), 86 (B), 89 (B);
Richard Shiell: p. 71 (C), 79 (B);
Pam Spaulding/Positive Images: p. 69 (B);
The Studio Central: p. 32, 36, 42 (T, B, B inset), 43 (B),
    47, 48 (dropouts), 49, 63 (C), 67;
The Toro Company: p. 42 (T inset);
Michael S. Thompson: p. 20, 21 (C), 23 (T), 64 (T),
    72 (T), 74 (C), 75 (T);
Steven Trusty: p. 25, 43 (T);
J.B. Unruh: p. 76 (R);
Tom Voigt: 74 (T);
Tom Watschke: p. 88 (C);
Ron West: p. 79 (T, C), 81 (C, B).

Note to the Readers: Due to differing conditions,
tools, and individual skills, Meredith Corporation assumes
no responsibility for any damages, injuries suffered, or losses
incurred as a result of following the information
published in this book. Before beginning any project, review
the instructions carefully, and if any doubts or questions
remain, consult local experts or authorities. Always read and
observe all of the safety precautions provided by
manufacturers of any tools, equipment, or supplies, and
follow all accepted safety procedures.

Cover photo: Walter Chandoha

WHAT MAKES A GREAT LAWN?

There's nothing like a lawn. Its scent and texture inspires feelings of comfort and safety.

There's nothing like a lawn. Large or small, urban or suburban, lawns are irreplaceable pieces of the fabric of American life. Our lawns are the welcome mats to our homes. They present our best face to visitors and neighbors. They frame our houses. They cradle our children. They connect our property with our neighbor's but serve also as our private green space.

Lawns give us daily contact with nature and are a symbol of our care. When well-kept, they are a sign of our commitment to order in the neighborhood.

We ask a lot from lawns. We demand that they look good while we use them hard for entertaining, relaxing, and playing. This use—and abuse—is a challenge for the plants in the lawn, the turfgrasses. Yet, no other plant is as versatile or as well suited to this task.

Turfgrasses cushion our steps, absorb noise, and cool the air. They prevent erosion and

Lawns are vital elements in the design of home landscapes. That patch of grass is open space that contrasts with beds. However, because of its flat, horizontal, nature, it doesn't compete with other plants for attention but instead provides a background for them.

Lawns serve as natural cushioning carpets around our homes, providing the safest playing surfaces for kids.

reduce pollution. They take constant abuse, and keep coming back for more.

It's true that in recent years, turfgrass has come under attack as a high maintenance plant that requires large inputs of water, chemicals, and work. But these days that is not necessarily true. Research and real-world experience have shown that turf gets by with less water, fertilizer, and even less mowing than once thought possible.

New varieties require much less overall maintenance than ones that were popular just a few years ago. That's good, because as much as we love our lawns, most of us wouldn't mind spending a bit less time tending them and a bit more time enjoying them.

It's difficult to imagine life without lawns. Their aesthetic value is integral to the landscape; they are design elements that provide open, horizontal space. They lead the eye (and the feet) to the other aspects of our yards: trees, shrubs, flower beds, and hardscaping.

Even the smallest lawn opens a landscape on which we can stand and stroll, and from which we view and gain perspective on our immediate surroundings. In the progression of our plantings, the lawn gives us pause. In the art of the landscape, it is the canvas upon which we paint.

Beyond its practical and aesthetic value, the lawn seems to satisfy us emotionally. It possesses a somehow indefinable quality that brings us comfort and makes it a refuge.

It does all this, provided that we're not worn out and frustrated by tending it. But lawn care does not have to be a difficult chore. It's not all that complicated.

In fact, with a basic understanding of the plants in your lawn—their habits and requirements—you'll find that lawn care is not a chore at all.

THE COST OF A LAWN

There are approximately 30,000,000 acres of lawn in the United States. Fifty-three million households have lawns, ranging from tiny plots to huge acreages.

Homeowners spend more than $5 billion a year on lawn care supplies, equipment, and services. They put in about 40 hours per year tending their lawns, at an average cost of $327 yearly.

Starting a new lawn costs about $70 per 1,000 square feet, with more than 80 percent of that cost going into labor and equipment. Fertilizer and lime account for about 8 percent of the total, and seed costs represent the smallest portion—only about 4 percent.

GRASS ANATOMY

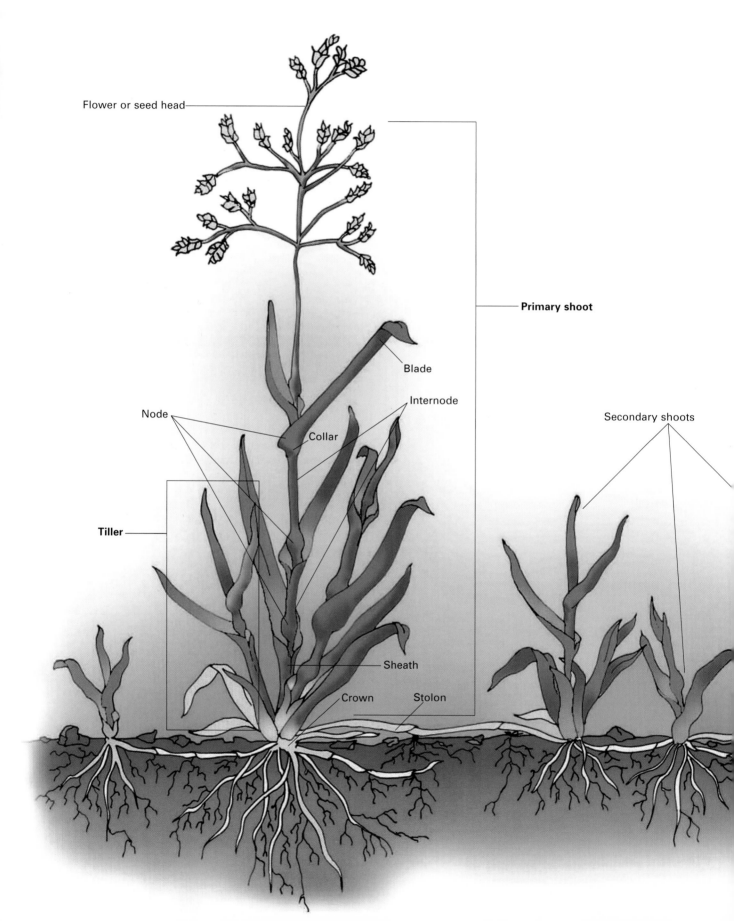

Flower or seed head

Primary shoot

Blade

Internode

Node

Collar

Secondary shoots

Tiller

Sheath

Crown   Stolon

Grass is a survivor, an ancient plant that evolved over millions of years in sun-filled prairies and meadows, where large animals grazed on it. The densely formed grasses that survived in these ancient ecosystems were the ones with crowns that hugged the ground—out of the grazers' reach. The heritage and genetic makeup of these grasses have served them well. The turfgrasses in our lawns today are descendants of those early plants.

Although many of us spend plenty of time maintaining and enjoying our lawns—mowing them, fertilizing them, and just playing on the grasses—few of us ever examine the plants themselves. If we ever did take a closer look, we would be amazed by their intricacy and variety.

All turfgrasses grow from a ground-hugging growth point, an area at the base of the plant called the *crown*. Today, except for the occasional rabbit, animals no longer graze on the grasses in our lawn. Our mowers clip them instead, but as long as the crown is not damaged, the plant will survive.

Roots and *shoots* originate from the crown. Below ground, the fibrous root system, whose length can vary considerably from one species to another, absorbs nutrients and water from the soil and anchors the plant. Above ground, stems and leaves take in light and carbon dioxide.

Extending upward from the crown, the *primary shoot* is the first to develop from a

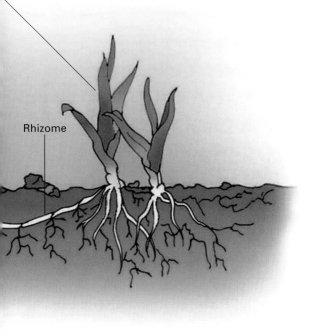

Rhizome

germinating seed. It—and every subsequent shoot—consists of leaves borne on short stems. A leaf consists of a *blade* and a *sheath*, the blade being the broad upper portion, and the sheath the lower portion that encircles the stem. The sheath remains wrapped around the stem while the blade unfurls and grows upward.

The sheath and blade meet at a point called the *collar*. Inside the collar is the *ligule*, a thin membranous band or ring of hairs, which ends in ear-like lobes called *auricles*. Together, the size, shape and makeup of ligules and auricles provide valuable clues for identifying a grass.

Both the blades and sheaths originate from *nodes*, which are bulbous joints on stems. There are several nodes on each stem (including spreading stems), and the portions between them are called *internodes*. Several blades, sheaths, nodes and internodes can exist on a primary shoot. Nodes and internodes don't really show up until the grass plant starts to flower, then the internodes begin to elongate. Timely mowing prevents flowering, keeping internodes compact.

Tillers are secondary shoots that also grow from the crown. As they expand, they help make a lawn thick and full. All grasses exhibit some tiller growth, but the class that is known as *bunch grasses* have especially heavy tiller activity. Because of these plentiful tillers arising from the crown, bunch grasses, such as chewings, hard and tall fescues, and the ryegrasses, form thick clumps as they expand and fill a lawn.

Other grasses, called *creeping grasses,* spread primarily by specialized stems—rhizomes and stolons—that extend horizontally from the crown of the parent plant.

Rhizomes are creeping stems that travel below ground while *stolons* (or runners) travel above ground. Some creeping grasses, such as Kentucky bluegrass and red fescue, spread by rhizomes; some, such as centipedegrass and St. Augustinegrass, spread by stolons; still others, such as bermudagrass and zoysiagrass, spread by both rhizomes and stolons.

As they grow, stolons and rhizomes produce new plants at their nodes, each with its own set of roots. A *secondary shoot*, similar to the primary shoot of the parent plant, develops when a node on a rhizome or stolon roots and sprouts.

The incredible turfgrass plant is unlike anything else in your landscape. Understanding its structure and growth is the first step in building a foundation for high-quality lawn care.

CLASSES OF GRASSES

Turfgrasses can be classified according to their botanical differences, but on a practical level, it is useful to consider them in terms of the climates they prefer and the times of year in which they grow best. They fall into two categories: cool and warm. Each has a seasonal period of growth when it is best to do major maintenance activities, such as dethatching.

Cool-season grasses thrive in areas 1, 3, 4, and 5 on the map below. Warm-season grasses are best adapted in areas 2, 7, and 8. Area 6 is a transition zone where both warm- and cool-season grasses will grow, though it's not a preferred climate for either group.

COOL SEASON VS. WARM SEASON

Cool-season grasses grow well in the northern United States above the bluegrass line, a climactic zone that runs roughly across the northern sections of North Carolina, Tennessee, Arkansas, Oklahoma, and Texas, then through New Mexico and Arizona to the Pacific Ocean (areas 1, 3, 4, and 5 on the map). They perform well at high elevations and along the mild, dry, coastal belts of California. In snowy climates they go dormant during winter. The most commonly grown species of cool-season grasses include bentgrasses, Kentucky bluegrass, fine fescues, tall fescues, and perennial ryegrass.

By nature, cool-season grasses grow actively in cool spring weather and slow down or go dormant in the heat of summer. Periods of drought during the warmer months bring on dormancy, but with regular watering, they often will stay green through the growing season. In areas with hot summers, they usually must be grown with irrigation.

Most warm-season grasses do not thrive in cool climates. They are best adapted to the southern part of the United States, below the "bluegrass line," and to other areas with hot summers and mild winters (areas 2, 6, 7, and 8 on the map). The most common warm-season grasses are bermudagrass, St. Augustinegrass, zoysiagrass, bahiagrass, carpetgrass, and centipedegrass. The actual levels of hardiness (tolerance to cold) of warm-season grasses varies considerably. Buffalograss and blue gramagrass, for example, are generally considered warm-season grasses but will tolerate colder climates than other warm-season varieties.

Warm-season grasses grow most vigorously during the warm summer months. Their winter behavior depends on the species and location. Some undergo dormancy and turn

TURFGRASS CLIMATE MAP

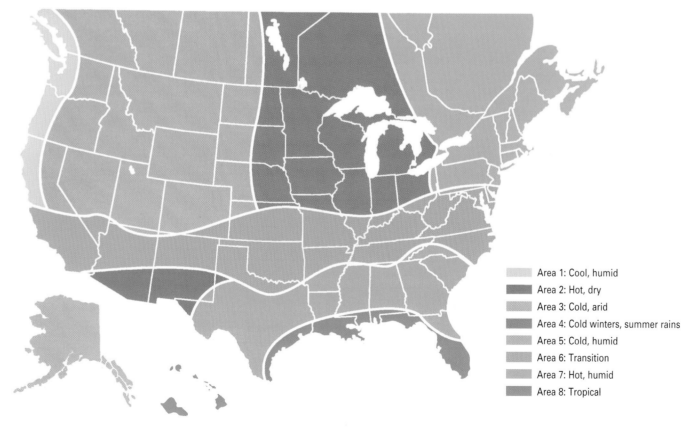

Area 1: Cool, humid
Area 2: Hot, dry
Area 3: Cold, arid
Area 4: Cold winters, summer rains
Area 5: Cold, humid
Area 6: Transition
Area 7: Hot, humid
Area 8: Tropical

brown or yellow in fall or winter. Others are not hardy enough to survive the cold. Still others, particularly those grown in mild coastal climates, may stay green all year.

Of course, the border between the warm-season zones and the cool-season zones is not a hard and fast one. In the transition zone (area 6), both warm and cool season grasses can be grown with varying degrees of success. How well they grow depends on specific microclimates, land elevation, heat, cold, and rainfall amounts. When in doubt, it's a good idea to check with your local extension service or garden center for guidance in determining which type of grass will grow best in your lawn.

Cool season grasses, such as the Kentucky bluegrass shown here, are at their best in the North, where summers are relatively cool and moist. They thrive—growing fast, thick and green—during spring, and again in autumn.

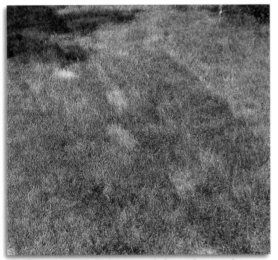

During summer's heat and drought, cool-season grasses, such as Kentucky bluegrass, may show signs of stress. Without regular watering, they turn brown and go dormant.

PRACTICAL CONSIDERATIONS

Warm-season grasses grow best when the weather is warm— in late spring through summer and into early fall. Cool-season grasses do best in the cool temperatures of spring and fall. Let this seasonality of growth guide you to the best times for major lawn maintenance projects.

Whenever tackling activities that essentially "tear up" the grass, such as dethatching, aerifying or renovating the lawn, do them either early in the period of most active growth or just before growth starts. Scheduling these jobs early in the grass's season allows the turf to recover and fill in before the temperature changes for the worst for the grass.

The times to work on cool-season grasses are early spring or late summer to early fall. Early to midsummer is best for warm-season grasses. When renovating cool-season lawns, be aware that competition from germinating weed seeds is lowest in late summer to early fall, so this may be the best time to schedule this task.

Warm-season grasses, such as zoysiagrass, left, grow vigorously and stay green during the heat of summer. However, during cool weather, they stop growing and go dormant. Zoysiagrass is especially slow to green up in spring and quick to turn brown in fall, right.

CLASSES OF GRASSES
continued

Both warm-season and cool-season grasses can be further categorized by the way they grow, their life span, and appearance.

BUNCH GRASSES VS. CREEPING GRASSES

As explained earlier, turfgrasses employ two distinct means of spreading: tillering and creeping. Bunch grasses, such as annual and perennial ryegrass, blue gramagrass, and tall fescue, expand by growing tillers from their crowns. A bunch-grass lawn is a collection of individual plants growing in tufts or bunches.

Creeping grasses, such as bentgrass, Kentucky bluegrass, and bermudagrass, spread by sending out rhizomes and stolons. Creeping grasses exhibit some tiller growth, but expand primarily with creeping stems that root and give rise to new plants. Consequently, a lawn of creeping grass is a thickly knit mat of mother and daughter plants.

Virtually all warm-season grasses are creeping grasses. Their extensive root system helps them survive the stress of heat and drought.

The cool-season category includes bunch grasses and creeping grasses, and the two types are often combined in northern grass seed mixtures and lawns.

PERENNIAL VS. ANNUAL

Most of the commonly grown turfgrasses are perennial. They live and continue to grow and spread year after year. They may slip into dormancy during winter and during times of stress from drought or cold, but they spring back to life and resume growing vigorously when conditions improve.

Annual grasses live for only one season. There are only a few annual turfgrasses, the most notable being annual ryegrass. Although annual grasses, especially annual ryegrass, are often used as a component in inexpensive grass seed mixes, they have little value in a permanent lawn. However, because they germinate and grow quickly, they can be used as a temporary lawn. In mild winter areas, turf growers often use them to overseed the dormant warm-season grasses for winter color.

FINE TEXTURED VS. COARSE TEXTURED

Grasses can also be categorized by their blade width. Those with blades that measure ¼ inch or narrower are known as fine-textured grasses, and they form the basis for a good-looking, refined lawn. They include creeping red bentgrass, Kentucky bluegrass, buffalograss, and zoysiagrass.

Creeping grasses, such as Kentucky bluegrass, above, spread quickly by stolons or rhizomes.

Bunch grasses grow in slowly spreading clumps. Mixes of bunch and creeping grasses often become weedy looking.

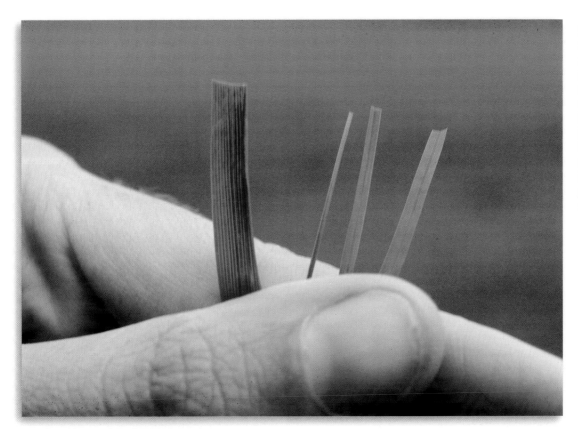

Blade width can vary considerably among turfgrass species as shown by the blades of, from left to right, tall fescue, fine fescue, Kentucky bluegrass and perennial ryegrass.

Grasses with blades wider than ¼ inch are called coarse or rough textured. Some of these grasses, such as common or KY-31 tall fescue, and varieties of perennial ryegrass, are not far removed in appearance from their pasture-grass parentage. With good maintenance, these grasses form nice lawns. However, they're not for everyone.

Over the years, turfgrass breeders have worked to improve the texture of many of these coarse varieties. Not long ago, for example, tall fescue existed only as a very coarse-bladed grass. But new varieties, known as turf-type tall fescues, have fine blades rivaling those of Kentucky bluegrass.

There is another aesthetic quality of grasses that we look for but do not categorize: color. In our current culture, we favor deep green lawns. The greener the better. That's one of the main reasons we fertilize. Color also is genetically determined; some species are naturally a much deeper green color than others. And breeders are taking advantage of that fact to develop new dark green varieties.

PRACTICAL CONSIDERATIONS

Establishment: Bunch grasses spread slower than most creeping grasses, and are usually sown at a heavier rate to compensate. Creeping grasses grown from plugs or sprigs, such as hybrid bermudagrass and zoysiagrass, are slow spreaders, too. They may take a full season or longer to cover the ground. Be vigilant about keeping the lawn free of weeds until these grasses become established.

Wear tolerance: In general, bunch grasses are more durable, resisting wear and tear. If your family is hard on a lawn, using it for football games and other such activities, a bunch grass such as perennial ryegrass or turf-type tall fescue may be best. However, creeping grasses often recover from injury faster.

Permanence: Your lawn should consist almost entirely of perennial grasses. But you can sow annual ryegrass for a temporary cover until your permanent lawn can be sown or sodded. In winter, you can also seed annual ryegrass over dormant warm-season grasses for all-season color.

Aesthetics: Texture considerations are primarily aesthetic. Some coarse-textured grasses make a lawn look rough, especially if mixed with finer textured varieties. Others, such as St. Augustinegrass and tall fescue, are widely used in highly aesthetic situations. If you expect your lawn to be a showcase, and your patch of turf is more often viewed than used, go with a fine-bladed, creeping grass such as Kentucky bluegrass.

GALLERY OF GRASSES

Growing just the right grass in just the right place is the most important step in making a fine lawn. Turfgrass species vary considerably in climactic, environmental, and cultural preferences. Chances are there's one that's just right for your lawn, or even that corner you've had so much trouble with.

Maybe it's the grass variety you're growing now. Maybe another species would do better. In either case, whether you're improving your care program to match your lawn or starting a new lawn, you need information.

And that's what you'll find in the gallery of grasses on this and the following pages. You'll find clues to help you identify the major grass species as well as discussions of their strengths and weaknesses, along with recommendations for the best varieties.

We start with cool season grasses and continue with warm season species on page 20.

good component in shady lawn mixtures. In the South, it is often used successfully to overseed warm-season grasses to provide winter color.

CANADA BLUEGRASS (*Poa compressa*) is a cold-tolerant, fine-textured creeping bluegrass. As its botanical name suggests, it can be distinguished by its flattened stems. Its common name gives a clue to its natural growing range: It is well adapted to Canada and the northern United States.

Recommended as a low-maintenance turf, Canada bluegrass can survive even in very poor soil. Although this species was once considered a lawn weed because it tends to form thin turf, new cultivars demonstrate much better density and vigor. Canada bluegrass is a good substitute for high-maintenance turf in conservation areas, on banks, and in hard-to-access areas.

ANNUAL BLUEGRASS (*Poa annua*), a low-growing, creeping grass, is a weed. Stay away from any seed mixtures containing it.

KENTUCKY BLUEGRASS

- Ligule
- Leaf tip
- Collar

Blade: V-shaped; boat-shaped tip. Ligule: Clear, cropped. Collar: Smooth, yellowish-green. New leaf: Folded.

BLUEGRASS

Kentucky bluegrass (*Poa pratensis*) is a cool-season, creeping, fine-textured perennial with good color and vigorous spreading ability. Its appearance is the standard against which all other turfgrasses are measured.

Bluegrass was one of the first turfgrasses to be grown in the early lawns of America, and today it is widely used for lawns, parks, athletic fields, golf fairways, and general purpose turf. Very cold tolerant, it is best adapted to the northern states east of the Rockies and to the Pacific Northwest, but it also is widely grown in the cool areas and higher elevations of the South. (The Plains states are often too dry for a satisfactory bluegrass lawn.)

KENTUCKY BLUEGRASS has unjustly acquired the reputation of being a high-maintenance grass. It's true that older, common Kentucky bluegrass, and some of the older improved varieties, were prone to disease. They required high inputs of fertilizer and water to maintain their green color through the growing season. New cultivars, however, have good disease resistance, and retain their fine appearance without heavy fertilization and watering.

ROUGH BLUEGRASS (*Poa trivialis*) is a bright-green, fine-textured, shallow-rooted relative of Kentucky bluegrass. Although it is not as versatile as its high-class cousin, it makes a good substitute in moist soils and shade. The grass is soft-bladed, and in mild climates, retains its color over winter. Because it can survive without full sun, it makes a

Rough bluegrass

Kentucky bluegrass

BLUEGRASS CULTURE

KENTUCKY BLUEGRASS
■ Sow 1–2 pounds of seed per 1,000 square feet. (Because Kentucky bluegrass germinates slowly, seed mixes often contain other faster-germinating grasses such as perennial ryegrass.)
■ Mow at 1½–2½ inches.
■ Fertilize with 2–3 pounds of nitrogen per 1,000 square feet.

ROUGH BLUEGRASS
■ Sow 2–3 pounds of seed per 1,000 square feet. For winter overseeding in the South, sow 15–20 pounds per 1,000 square feet.
■ Mow at 2–3 inches.
■ Fertilize with 1–2 pounds of nitrogen per 1,000 square feet.

CANADA BLUEGRASS
■ Sow 2–4 pounds of seed per 1,000 square feet.
■ Mow at 3–4 inches.
■ Fertilize with 2–3 pounds of nitrogen per 1,000 square feet.

PROS AND CONS

Kentucky bluegrass is perhaps the cold-hardiest of all turfgrass, making a dependable lawn in the northern reaches of the United States. Wherever it grows, it's noted for its fine texture and dense, thick turf. Though new varieties have some drought tolerance, Kentucky bluegrass requires regular watering to maintain its bright color through hot, dry seasons. It also needs more fertilizing and more frequent mowing than many other cool-season grasses. It does not tolerate shade. Kentucky bluegrass was once considered disease prone, but most new varieties have good resistance.

Rough bluegrass grows well in shade, but does not tolerate full sun and drought.

Canada bluegrass survives in infertile and acidic soils, high elevations and cool temperatures. It can go for long periods without mowing. However, this species is not suited for fine turf.

BLUEGRASS CULTIVARS

KENTUCKY BLUEGRASS
'America': low growing; good density; resistant to stripe smut, leaf spot, powdery mildew, fusarium blight, and rust.
'Blacksburg': dwarf habit; dark blue-green color; good density; widely adaptable.
'Blue Star': rich emerald-green; early spring greenup, holds color late into fall; drought tolerant; good in ryegrass or fescue blends or in bluegrass mixes; disease resistant.
'Chateau': deep green color; thick, dense turf; early spring greenup, holds color well into fall; moderately shade tolerant; good in blends with ryegrass, fescue, turf-type tall fescue or in bluegrass mixes; resistant to most turf diseases.
'Coventry': medium dark green; dense, medium-textured turf; excellent winter hardiness; good tolerance to rust, dollar spot and summer patch diseases.
'Eclipse': light green, moderately dense, medium-textured turf; grows vigorously to form dense turf; resistant to stripe smut, fusarium blight, and rust; shade tolerant.

'Glade': dark green; very good density; fine texture; tolerates light shade; good resistance to leaf spot, stripe smut, and powdery mildew.
'Julia': moderately dark green; medium texture; upright growth; good spring and fall color; excellent density and wear tolerance; resists leaf spot, stem rust, and melting out.
'Midnight': dark blue-green color; excellent turf, widely adaptable across the United States; resistant to stripe smut, dollar and leaf spot; very good heat and cold tolerance.

ROUGH BLUEGRASS
'Colt': light green, forms moderately dense turf.
'Cypress': excellent dark green color; very fine texture; adapted as perennial in colder regions.
'Sabre': dark green; low growing, dense turf; well adapted to cool, moist climates; germinates rapidly.

CANADA BLUEGRASS
'Reubens': short, stiff, fine blades and dark green color; improved vigor and better density than the species.

Lawn grasses rarely come in a bag as a single species; instead, they're sold as mixtures and blends (see page 61). When buying seed, check the label to see whether the bag contains these or other improved cultivars.

GLOSSARY

As you do your turfgrass homework, you'll find a few descriptive terms repeated. Here's what they mean.
Low maintenance: A maintenance regime in which fertilizer, water, and mowing are at much lower than optimum rates.
High maintenance: A maintenance regime that provides optimum, or better than optimum, amounts of water and fertilizer combined with frequent mowing.
Tolerates low mowing: The ability of a variety to tolerate a much shorter mowing height than other varieties in the species while retaining color and vigor.
Tolerates infrequent mowing: The ability of a variety to grow slow enough to need little mowing or to look fine even when allowed to reach 3 or 4 inches tall.
Disease resistance: The ability of a variety to thrive despite the presence of disease-causing fungi.
Wear tolerance: The ability of a variety to tolerate frequent foot or other type of traffic.
Spring greenup: The time when a variety breaks dormancy.
Density: The number of shoots in an area: the greater the number, the denser, or thicker, the turf.

GALLERY OF GRASSES
continued

FINE FESCUES

Fine fescues, which include chewings, hard, red (sometimes called creeping red), and sheep fescues, are fine-bladed grasses. They are used extensively in seed blends and mixes for both sunny and shady situations.

Some fine fescue varieties will germinate and become established quickly. Medium green in color, some spread by tillers, others by short, creeping rhizomes. Fine fescues don't like heat, and during extended, hot, dry periods, they may lose their color rapidly.

Though members of this family behave similarly, there are differences among them. **CHEWINGS FESCUE** (*Festuca rubra commutata*) is an aggressive, bunch-type fine fescue that can overtake other grasses. That's good for crowding out weeds but not for maintaining other grasses. It is sometimes used to overseed shady lawns, often in mixtures with perennial ryegrass or Kentucky bluegrass.

Chewings fescue is adapted to cooler areas in the northern United States and Canada, and to the coastal regions of the Northeast and Pacific Northwest. Elsewhere it is best suited to areas where summers are cool.

Because it is moderately wear-tolerant and well adapted to sandy, acidic, and infertile soils in these regions, chewings fescue is a good choice for a low-maintenance turf in shaded, low-traffic areas in parks and lawns.

HARD FESCUE (*Festuca longifolia*) is a fine-textured grass grown mostly at high elevations in the northern United States and Canada. It has gained popularity lately as a strong low-maintenance grass. It requires low fertilization and its short growth and slow growth rate mean less frequent mowings.

Growing in clumps, hard fescue is slower to become established than chewings fescue and red fescue, but it needs minimal maintenance when mature. It has thin, firm leaves, but it does not form rhizomes, making it somewhat less resistant to wear. It is very well suited to covering slopes and banks.

RED FESCUE (*Festuca rubra*), also known as creeping red fescue, is often combined with Kentucky bluegrass in good-quality lawn seed mixes. A fine-textured, low-maintenance grass with narrow, dark green blades, it blends well and does what most bluegrasses cannot— it grows well in shade and drought. It is preferable to chewings fescue in a seed mix because it is more wear tolerant and is less likely to form thatch.

Red fescue has a creeping growth habit, spreading by rhizomes and tillers. It is best adapted where summers are cool, such as in the coastal Northwest and at high elevations, and it is widely planted in the Great Lakes region.

Growing well on banks and slopes, red fescue creates an especially lush effect when left unmowed. It is also good for overseeding dormant warm-season grasses in winter, provided that the site isn't heavily trafficked.

CHEWINGS FESCUE

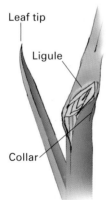

Leaf tip

Ligule

Collar

Blade: Folded; boat-shaped tip.
Ligule: Clear, short.
Collar: Smooth.
New leaf: Folded.

Sheep fescue   *Chewings fescue*   *Hard fescue*

Red fescue

SHEEP FESCUE (*Festuca ovina*) is a cool-season perennial bunch grass that requires little water. Once established, it is persistent and winter hardy.

Though it does not make an elegant lawn, sheep fescue is a good low-maintenance grass for off-the-beaten-path areas in public parks and lawns. Improved varieties have deep blue-green, finely textured foliage.

Sheep fescue does well in cool dry areas and requires infrequent mowing and minimal fertilizer.

FINE FESCUE CULTURE

CHEWINGS FESCUE AND RED FESCUE
- Sow 5 pounds of seed per 1,000 square feet.
- Mow at 1½–2½ inches.
- Fertilize with 1–2 pounds of nitrogen per 1,000 square feet per year.

HARD FESCUE
- Sow 5 pounds of seed per 1,000 square feet.
- Mow at 1½–2½ inches or leave unmown in conservation areas.
- Fertilize with 1–2 pounds of nitrogen per 1,000 square feet per year.

SHEEP FESCUE
- Sow 5 pounds of seed per 1,000 square feet.
- Mow at 2–4 inches, or leave unmown in conservation areas.
- Fertilize with 1–2 pounds of nitrogen per 1,000 square feet per year, though no fertilizer is necessary in low-maintenance areas.

PROS AND CONS

Chewings fescue is among the most shade tolerant of cool-season grasses. It is susceptible to disease when the weather is hot and wet, and it does not withstand heavy use well.

Hard fescue is shade and salt tolerant, and drought resistant. It requires less mowing and less fertilizer than other fescues, and it is highly resistant to many diseases. Its wearability is not especially good, and some older varieties are difficult to mow evenly, leaving the blade tips shredded and discolored.

Red fescue is very shade and drought tolerant, but it takes less heat than other fescues. It is susceptible to summer diseases in hot climates.

Sheep fescue is tolerant of a wide variety of soil types and can take partial shade, but it does not make a smooth turf.

FINE FESCUE CULTIVARS

CHEWINGS FESCUE
'Banner': dark green, good density, fine texture; tolerates mowing as low as 1 inch; moderately good disease resistance, but susceptible to powdery mildew.
'Banner II': attractive color; mildew, rust, and leaf spot resistant, good insect resistance.
'Bridgeport': dark green; grows upright; good disease and insect resistance; winter hardy; takes shade.
'Jamestown II': good color and texture; good insect resistance due to endophyte enhancement.
'SR 5000': low maintenance; takes dry, infertile, acid soils; shade tolerant; good disease and insect resistance.

HARD FESCUE
'Aurora': fine texture; dense, fine turf; good disease and wear resistance; drought tolerant.
'Biljart': low growth; tolerant of shade and heat.
'Brigade': medium-green leaves; good drought tolerance; maintains density under low levels of fertility and water; tolerates some shade.
'Gladiator': attractive color; low growing; good low-maintenance turf; shade tolerant; disease resistant.
'SR 3100': dark green; dwarf growth reduces mowing and maintenance; insect resistant.

RED FESCUE
'Claudia': dark green, fine texture, dense growth; good cold and shade tolerance; mixes well with Kentucky bluegrass and perennial ryegrass; resistant to red thread, summer patch, and pink patch.
'Ensylva': very fine leaved; vigorous; forms dense turf; good winter appearance and hardiness.
'Flyer': dark green color; shade and drought tolerant; disease resistant.
'Marker': very dark green; dense growth; tolerates low mowing; wear resistant.
'Medallion': dark green leaves; medium to tall height; good resistance to red thread and pink snow mold.
'Salem': dark green color; outstanding dense turf; early spring greenup; drought tolerant; resistant to leaf spot.
'Shademaster': bright, medium-green; good winter color and spring greenup; drought and shade tolerant; resistant to leaf spot, leaf rust, and powdery mildew.

SHEEP FESCUE
'Bighorn': powder-blue; improved uniformity and quality.
'SR 3000': fine, bright green leaves; dense growth; requires little to no water, fertilizer, or mowing; tolerates shade; good disease and insect resistance.

Lawn grasses rarely come in a bag as a single species; instead, they're sold as mixtures and blends (see page 61). When buying seed, check the label to see whether the bag contains these or other improved cultivars.

GALLERY OF GRASSES
continued

TALL FESCUE

Ligule

Leaf tip

Collar

**Blade: Broad, flat; blunt.
Ligule: Clear, long, cropped.
Collar: Hairy.
New leaf: Rolled.**

TALL FESCUE

Tall fescue (*Festuca arundinacea*), a dense clumping grass that is able to grow in sun or shade, is a good low-maintenance choice for home lawns, playing fields, and commercial grounds. It performs best in areas with mild winters and warm summers and in mild-temperature regions of the Southwest. It's one of the best turf choices for the transition zone. Where winters are mild, it will stay green all year.

Until recently, tall fescue was considered a poor grass for a good-looking lawn. The few available cultivars of tall fescue were coarse and pale colored, and they did not stand up well to wear. During the past several years, however, breeders have worked wonders with this species, and the new turf-type tall fescue varieties exhibit fine lawn qualities: good appearance, wearability, and low fertilizer requirements. Several of the turf-type tall fescues have fine-textured blades and good, rich color, as opposed to their coarser precursors.

Turf-type tall fescues tolerate high and infrequent mowing. Many of these varieties also demonstrate good disease and drought tolerance, and wearability. Some even resist damage from insects.

Turf-type tall fescue

Tall fescue

PROS AND CONS

Tall fescues prefer high mowing. In some areas, they grow rapidly in spring. New varieties stay green throughout the growing season with little fertilizer. Most are drought tolerant. Those qualities make tall fescue a good choice for low-maintenance lawns. However, most tall fescues do not mix well with other grasses, with the exception of non-aggressive bluegrass varieties. Older varieties such as 'Kentucky 31' and 'Alta' are light-colored and coarse textured, lending a weedy appearance to lawns with fine turfgrasses.

TALL FESCUE CULTURE

■ Sow 8–10 pounds of seed per 1,000 square feet. Germinates within 7–10 days.
■ Mow at 1½–3 inches.
■ Fertilize with 1–2 pounds of nitrogen per 1,000 square feet per year (3–4 pounds in areas with long growing seasons).

TALL FESCUE CULTIVARS

'Amigo': dense; dwarf habit; bright green color; slow-growing, upright foliage; shade tolerant; resistant to brown patch and pythium blight.
'Cimarron': dark green color; low-growing, moderately fine textured, dense turf; disease resistant; very good heat, cold, wear and shade tolerance.
'Ninja': dark green, fine blades, dense; slow growth; withstands low mowing, heavy traffic; resists red thread and fusarium wilt, brown patch, pythium, blight, and leaf spot; tolerates heat, cold, and drought; blends well with bluegrass and perennial ryegrass.
'Rebel II': medium- to low-maintenance turf in full sun or light to moderate shade; dark green color; fine texture; disease resistant; tolerant of heat and close mowing.
'Twilight': blue-green color; moderately coarse texture; moderately dense turf.
'Wrangler': moderately low-growing semidwarf with medium-dark green color and texture; good disease resistance; good shade tolerance.

Lawn grasses rarely come in a bag as a single species; instead, they're sold as mixtures and blends (see page 61). When buying seed, check the label to see whether the bag contains these or other improved cultivars.

Perennial ryegrass

RYEGRASS

PERENNIAL RYEGRASS (*Lolium perenne*) exhibits the best wear tolerance of any cool-season grass, which is why it's commonly selected to plant on playing fields and well-used home lawns. Like tall fescue, it has received a lot of attention from turf breeders. The result has been new, moderate- to high-maintenance turf-type perennial ryegrass varieties that are fine bladed, rich green, and resistant to pests and diseases.

Perennial ryegrass can be grown successfully throughout the cool-season turfgrass regions and in cooler parts and higher elevations of the warm-season region. It is not as cold tolerant as Kentucky bluegrass or as drought tolerant as tall fescue.

Perennial ryegrass likes full sun, but will tolerate some shade. Its non-creeping, bunch-type growth forms a uniform lawn if it is properly maintained.

ANNUAL RYEGRASS (*Lolium multiflorum*), also known as Italian ryegrass, is a cool-season annual grass that forms a medium- to coarse-textured lawn with moderate wear resistance. Though seed of annual rye is often found in inexpensive grass mixes, it does not belong in a permanent lawn because it only lives for one year. In temperate areas, it is sometimes used as temporary lawn, and in mild-winter areas of the South and West it is often overseeded on dormant warm-season grasses to provide winter color.

PERENNIAL RYEGRASS

Ligule

Leaf tip

Collar

Blade: Flat; sharp tip.
Ligule: Clear, long, cropped.
Collar: Narrow.
New leaf: Folded.

RYEGRASS CULTURE

PERENNIAL RYEGRASS
■ Sow 5–10 pounds of seed per 1,000 square feet.
■ Mow at 1½–2½ inches.
■ Fertilize with 2–3 pounds of fertilizer per 1,000 square feet per year (4–6 pounds in areas with long seasons).

ANNUAL RYEGRASS
■ Sow 5–10 pounds of seed per 1,000 square feet (10–20 pounds per 1,000 square feet for overseeding).
■ Mow at 1½–2½ inches.
■ Fertilize with 2–3 pounds of nitrogen per 1,000 square feet per year.

PROS AND CONS

Perennial ryegrass is a good low-maintenance choice for home lawns subject to a lot of wear and traffic. It can be mowed closely or left to grow long. New varieties have more insect resistance than any other species but require a higher level of maintenance. Perennial ryegrass does not do well in shade, extreme cold or heat and drought. Annual ryegrass germinates extremely quickly and can be used to establish temporary lawns.

PERENNIAL RYEGRASS CULTIVARS

'Advent': rich green color; fine texture; low, dense growth; excellent heat and drought tolerance; good disease resistance.

'Calypso': dark green; fine texture; good wear tolerance; resists leaf spot, brown patch, and dollar spot.

'Delaware Dwarf': dark green; fine texture; low growth habit, reduced growth rate; excellent for overseeding in the South; high level of endophytes for insect resistance.

'Manhattan II': dark green foliage with fine texture; good plant density; tolerant of compacted soil; germinates quickly; resistant to brown patch, crown rust, and stem rust.

'Nobility': attractive, dark green color; fine texture from very narrow blade; mows easily; good resistance to damage from wilting and excellent drought recovery; slow-growth habit allows infrequent mowing; high endophyte level for good insect resistance.

'Pennant': medium-dark green leaves with medium-fine texture and good density; good heat and cold tolerance; very winter hardy; resistant to brown patch and red thread.

'Repell': leafy and persistent; good shade tolerance; resistant to fusarium blight and brown patch; good resistance to cutworms, sod webworms, armyworm, billbugs and chinch bugs.

Lawn grasses rarely come in a bag as a single species; instead, they're sold as mixtures and blends (see page 61). When buying seed, check the label to see whether the bag contains these or other improved cultivars.

GALLERY OF GRASSES
continued

Bentgrass

CREEPING BENTGRASS

Leaf tip

Ligule

Collar

**Blade: Narrow, flat, broadly pointed.
Ligule: Clear, pointed, long.
Collar: Narrow.
New leaf: Rolled.**

BENTGRASS

The bentgrasses are the finest-bladed, lowest-growing, and highest-maintenance species of all the cool-season turfgrasses. It's true they make a fine-looking lawn, but they require a great deal of care—frequent mowing, watering, and fertilizing.

Their distinctive growth habit and color do not mix well with other grasses. They are susceptible to many diseases. On the positive side, there are species well adapted to small regions of the country where they can survive with less care.

CREEPING BENTGRASS (*Agrostis palustris*) is the finest-textured and lowest-growing of all. This is the grass that's used on putting and bowling greens. It forms a soft, dense carpet-like lawn, but requires good drainage and frequent watering. It also requires good air flow over the surface of the lawn to prevent disease. It will tolerate some shade.

COLONIAL BENTGRASS (*A. tenuis*) is a bit more user friendly. It tolerates higher mowing and less fertilizer. When mowed closely it forms a dense turf. If left unmown, it can serve as a conservation grass, stabilizing banks. It is well adapted to the Pacific Northwest.

REDTOP (*A. alba*) often is included in inexpensive cool-season and construction-grade mixes because it germinates and spreads rapidly. Be aware that while they are growing, the coarse plants often out-compete other, more desirable grasses.

BUFFALOGRASS

One of only two native grasses grown as turf in North America, buffalograss (*Buchloe dactyloides*) has fine-textured, curling blades with outstanding heat tolerance. Gray-green from late spring to hard frost, this warm-season grass turns straw colored through its dormancy in late fall and winter. It does well in heavy soil, but prefers finer-textured soils.

Often planted for its low maintenance, buffalograss thrives in areas that receive only 12 to 25 inches of rain per year. This includes the region that stretches from Minnesota to central Montana, and south from Minnesota to Iowa, parts of Texas, and into northern Mexico.

Once one of the dominant grasses of the American prairie, buffalograss forms a matted, reasonably dense turf that takes hard wear and looks fairly good with little summer

BENTGRASS CULTURE

■ Sow 1 pound of seed per 1,000 square feet.
■ Mow frequently at ¼–¾ inch.
■ Fertilize with 2–6 pounds of nitrogen per 1,000 square feet per year.
■ Dethatch regularly.

PROS AND CONS

Though they make fine looking lawns and are tolerant of acid soils and light shade, bentgrasses are for the most part more trouble than they are worth. They require large amounts of fertilizer, water, pesticides, and frequent mowing and dethatching. The seeds are extremely small, so a well-prepared seed bed is required, and the grass is slow to become established from seed. Colonial bentgrass, however, can serve as a low-maintenance grass in areas of the Pacific Northwest.

BENTGRASS CULTIVARS

CREEPING BENTGRASS
'Lopez': dark green, medium-fine blades; good wear tolerance; resists scalping; greens up early in spring; blends well with other varieties.
'Penncross': fine texture; dense growth; good wear tolerance and disease resistance.

'Providence': dark green; fine; upright.
'Regent': medium-dark green color; fine texture; dense turf; superior disease resistance.
'Southshore': dark green; medium-fine; upright growth profile.

COLONIAL BENTGRASS:
'Bardot': dark green, narrow leaves; dense turf; good disease and drought resistance; suitable for low mowing and low-maintenance lawns.
'SR 7100': very fine textured; improved color retention and brown patch resistance.

Lawn grasses rarely come in a bag as a single species; instead, they're sold as mixtures and blends (see page 61). When buying seed, check the label to see whether the bag contains these or other improved cultivars.

A lawn of unmown buffalograss

Buffalograss

BUFFALOGRASS CULTURE

■ Sow 2 pounds of seed per 1,000 square feet; or plant 2-inch plugs at 1-foot intervals.
■ Mow at 2–3 inches if a conventional turf is desired, otherwise, leave unmown.
■ Fertilize with 1–2 pounds of nitrogen per 1,000 square feet.

PROS AND CONS

Though it needs little or no irrigation, fertilization, or watering, buffalograss does not meet everyone's expectations of a lawn. It makes a matted, reasonably dense turf, and its leaves are an off-green color. Though extremely drought and heat resistant, most buffalograss cultivars turn brown in extremely hot or cold temperatures. However, it can be mown to resemble turfgrass.

BUFFALOGRASS CULTIVARS

'609': dense growth; low growing.
'Bison': vigorous growth; dense turf.
'Buffalawn': vigorous growth.
'Cody': darker blue-green color than other varieties; very fine leaf texture; quick establishment; relatively drought tolerant.
'Texoka': very vigorous growth; forms dense turf.
'Topgun': good green color; dense plants; low growing; persistent; resistant to common root rot and nematodes.

Lawn grasses rarely come in a bag as a single species; instead, they're sold as mixtures and blends (see page 61). When buying seed, check the label to see whether the bag contains these or other improved cultivars.

Blade: Flat, gray-green, hairy.
Ligule: Long hairs.
Collar: Broad, smooth.
New leaf: Rolled.

watering. More lawn-like in appearance than other native grasses, it is becoming increasingly popular in drought-prone regions. Given minimal watering it grows slowly to 4 inches tall and requires little or no mowing.

Buffalograss does not compete well with aggressive grasses such as Kentucky bluegrass and bermudagrass, so those grasses, as well as grassy weeds such as quackgrass, should be eliminated before sowing buffalograss.

BLUE GRAMAGRASS

Blue gramagrass (*Bouteloua gracilis*) is another native of the prairies of the Great Plains. For years, it has been used as a pasture or conservation grass. However, it has been frequently put to use on lawns because it can serve as low-maintenance turf. Blue gramagrass is often mixed with buffalograss seed for a better looking lawn.

Grayish-green with fine-textured, curling leaves, blue gramagrass has excellent pest and disease resistance and tolerance to heat, cold, drought, and alkaline soils. Although technically a warm-season grass, it remains hardy to minus 40° F.

This grass spreads by short stolons and produces hairy leaves that grow in low tufts. Blue gramagrass can be left unmowed or, for a more turf-like appearance, mowed three to four times per year. Two varieties, 'Hachita' and 'Lovington', are produced principally for use on rangelands, but they also are suitable for low-maintenance, prairie-style lawns.

Blue gramagrass

BLUE GRAMAGRASS CULTURE

■ Sow 1–3 pounds of seed per 1,000 square feet.
■ Mow at 2–3 inches or leave unmown.
■ Fertilize with ½–1 pound of nitrogen per 1,000 square feet.

PROS AND CONS

Though extremely drought and heat resistant, the color of blue gramagrass is gray-green, turning brown in hot, dry weather. It does not form a thick turf. Because it germinates and establishes slowly, give it a head start—sow in early spring or in the fall.

Blade: Flat, hairy, broadly pointed.
Ligule: Short hairs.
Collar: Broad, hairy.
New leaf: Rolled.

GALLERY OF GRASSES
continued

ZOYSIAGRASS

Zoysiagrass (*Zoysia* species) is a tough, aggressive, creeping warm-season perennial with leaf texture that ranges from coarse to fine, depending on variety.

This is the grass that you often see advertised as a miracle grass, and it does have some outstanding characteristics. Tolerant of heat and drought yet able to endure some shade and cool temperatures, zoysiagrass forms a dense, wiry, low-maintenance lawn that crowds out weeds. However, the needlelike blades of many zoysiagrass can be sharp underfoot. And it tends to form a puffy turf.

Zoysiagrass is often grown in the transition zone between warm- and cool-season areas, and as far north as New Jersey in the East and Oregon in the West. In these areas it is at its best in the summer and competes well with warm-season weeds such as crabgrass. It will survive winters, but at the first hint of cold weather, zoysiagrass goes dormant and turns brown, while cool-season grasses are still bright green.

Three species are available. *Zoysia japonica* is the most vigorous and winter hardy, but its leaves are the coarsest. *Zoysia matrella* is not as winter hardy or as coarse. It is wear resistant and tolerates some shade. *Zoysia tenuifolia* is the least winter hardy but is the finest textured and the most attractive of the zoysiagrasses.

Older cultivars could not be propagated from seed, and lawns had to be started vegetatively from plugs. However, new, improved varieties may be grown from seed.

Zoysiagrass

Ligule   Leaf tip

Collar

Blade: Flat, stiff, hairy, pointed.
Ligule: Short hairs.
Collar: Broad, hairy.
New leaf: Rolled.

ZOYSIAGRASS CULTURE

ZOYSIAGRASS
■ Sow 1–2 pounds of hulled seed per 1,000 square feet (or plant 2-inch plugs 6 inches apart). Keep lawn weed free while grass becomes established.
■ Mow at ½–1 inch.
■ Fertilize with 2–3 pounds of nitrogen per 1,000 square feet per year.

PROS AND CONS

Zoysiagrass forms a dense turf that is resistant to weeds, insects and diseases. It does not aggressively invade garden beds like bermudagrass. However, it establishes slowly, browns out early in fall, and is slow to green up in spring.

Zoysiagrass does not mix well with other grasses in a lawn. Fine-leaved varieties tend toward a "fluffy" growth that often looks scalped when mown.

BAHIAGRASS

Bahiagrass (*Paspalum notatum*) is a tough, coarse-textured, moderately aggressive warm-season grass that is adapted to a wide range of soil conditions. It grows well in an area that stretches from the central coast of North Carolina, south to central and southern Florida, and west to eastern Texas.

Bahiagrass spreads slowly by short rhizomes. Once established, it becomes aggressive, quickly making a thick, low-maintenance turf. It has some drought resistance.

ZOYSIAGRASS, BAHIAGRASS, AND BERMUDAGRASS CULTIVARS

ZOYSIAGRASS
'Emerald': fine, dark green leaves; dense growth habit; adapted to the South.
'SR 9000': rapidly forming, uniform turf; low maintenance; can be blended with turf-type tall fescue.
'SR 9100': dense, low-growing, medium-textured turf.

BAHIAGRASS
'Pensacola': fine, glossy leaves; germinates quickly; cold tolerant.
'Wilmington': fine-textured and dark green leaves; very cold-tolerant; propagated by sprigs.

BERMUDAGRASS
'Midiron': bright to dark green color; medium-coarse texture; fast spreading; wear resistant.
'NuMex Sahara': medium-fine texture with dark green color; retains good color in summer; excellent drought tolerance; reduced plant height; good density; low in thatch; good seedling vigor; some resistance to bermuda-stunt mite.
'Sonesta': denser turf and finer texture than other bermudagrasses; good general purpose grass.
'Tifway II': dark green; dense turf; resistant to insects; good frost tolerance.

Lawn grasses rarely come in a bag as a single species; instead, they're sold as mixtures and blends (see page 61). When buying seed, check the label to see whether the bag contains these or other improved cultivars.

Because of its coarse blades and uneven growth, bahiagrass does not make an especially good-looking lawn, and the tough stems are difficult to mow evenly. Older, common bahiagrass is the coarsest of all and is susceptible to damage from temperatures below 20° F. Newer varieties are more cold tolerant and not as coarse.

A related variety, seashore paspalum (*P. vaginatum*) is a fine-textured bahiagrass that is tolerant of salty soils.

BERMUDAGRASS

Bermudagrass (*Cynodon* species) is to the South what Kentucky bluegrass is to the North—the stuff of which most lawns are made.

This creeping turfgrass is easily grown in most soils and takes both low and high maintenance regimes. Depending on the variety, bermudagrass resists many diseases and can take considerable wear and abuse. Deep roots allow it to tolerate heat and drought (although a bermudagrass lawn always looks better when it receives adequate water).

Bermudagrass grows throughout the warm-season turfgrass area, and well into some areas of the cool-season region. However, it is best adapted to lower elevations in the Southwest and in a region bounded by Maryland, Florida, Texas, and Kansas. When bermudagrass invades cool-season turf, it is considered a weed.

Older, common bermudagrass can be difficult to contain and keep out of areas where it is not wanted, such as flower borders and beds. Its vigorous growth rate also makes it prone to thatching, and it is subject to damage from insects and diseases.

It does not grow well in shade, and often goes dormant, turning yellow or brown, when fall temperatures drop below 50° to 60° F. Bermudagrass has been much improved in recent years, with new hybrid varieties that show improved texture and color, and drought, heat, and cold tolerance.

Softer, denser, and finer-textured than common bermudagrass, hybrid varieties are fast-growing, durable, heat-loving grasses used for everything from home lawns to golf courses. However, hybrid bermudagrass needs more sun, more fertilizer, and more frequent mowing than its common cousins. In fact, hybrid bermudagrass lawns should be mowed twice a week during their peak growth period in summer.

Many hybrid bermudagrass seeds are sterile so the turfgrass must be propagated by sod, sprigs, or stolons. However, some improved seeded varieties are available.

BAHIAGRASS CULTURE

BAHIAGRASS
■ Sow 6–10 pounds of seed per 1,000 square feet (or propagate by sprigs or sod).
■ Mow frequently at 2–3 inches.
■ Fertilize with 2–4 pounds of nitrogen per 1,000 square feet.

PROS AND CONS

Bahiagrass is somewhat shade and drought tolerant, and forms a thick turf that crowds out weeds without creating thatch. It grows well in sandy, slightly acid, infertile soil. However, bahiagrass needs frequent mowing to maintain good looks and is susceptible to brown patch, dollar spot, and mole crickets.

BERMUDAGRASS CULTURE

COMMON BERMUDAGRASS
■ Sow 1–2 pounds of seed per 1,000 square feet per year (up to 10 pounds in the South/Southwest). Seed germinates in 10–30 days.
■ Mow often at ½–1 inch.
■ Apply 1–4 pounds of nitrogen per 1,000 square feet per year.
HYBRID BERMUDAGRASS
■ Plant 2-inch sprigs 12 inches apart or 2 bushels of sprigs per 1,000 square feet.
■ Mow at ½–1 inch as often as twice weekly during peak growth periods.
■ Fertilize with 2–4 pounds of nitrogen per 1,000 square feet per year.

PROS AND CONS

Bermudagrass is a good-looking, dense, hard-working lawn for most of the South. It stands up to wear and tear and hot summer weather. However, bermudagrass's aggressive nature can work against it. It spreads by means of aggressive runners into flower beds, sidewalk cracks, etc. Bermudagrass is a relatively heavy feeder, and often requires irrigation to retain its color. Feeding and watering, in turn, increases the mowing required during summer. Bermudagrass may turn yellow if allowed to grow too long.

Bahiagrass

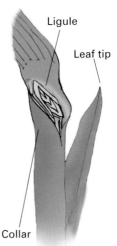

Blades: Flat or folded.
Ligule: Clear, cropped.
Collar: Broad.
New leaf: Rolled.

Bermudagrass

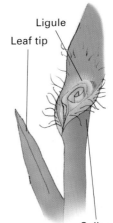

Blade: Rough, pointed.
Ligule: White hairs.
Collar: Narrow, smooth.
New leaf: Folded.

GALLERY OF GRASSES
continued

St. Augustinegrass

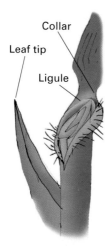

**Blade: Flat,
smooth, blunt.
Ligule: Short hairs.
Collar: Broad,
smooth.
New leaf: Folded.**

(diagram labels: Collar, Leaf tip, Ligule)

ST. AUGUSTINEGRASS

St. Augustinegrass (*Stenotaphrum secundatum*) is a robust, fast-growing, coarse-textured, warm-season perennial with broad, dark green blades. It spreads by means of stolons that root at the nodes and form a thick, dense turf that crowds out most weeds.

Suitable for lawns and other turfgrass areas where a fine texture is not required, St. Augustinegrass is among the most shade tolerant of warm-season grasses. Adapted to southern California, Hawaii, mild areas of the Southwest, Florida and other Gulf Coast states, a St. Augustinegrass lawn withstands heat well and is tolerant of salt spray and salty soil. On the minus side, it requires frequent watering and tends to lose its color as soon as the weather turns cold.

St. Augustinegrass is not low maintenance. It requires a fertile soil, one that is well-drained and rich in organic matter. Even in good soil, it requires regular fertilization with a high-nitrogen fertilizer. It is also susceptible to insect damage and diseases, including the viral St. Augustinegrass decline (SAD). Improved varieties offer resistance to disease and insect damage.

In spring and fall, St. Augustinegrass lawns grow slowly and require only twice-monthly mowing. During peak summer growth, it must be mowed at least weekly. Proper mowing height is critical. If mowed too low, weeds may get an upper hand. If allowed to grow too high between mowings, thatch may build up.

St. Augustinegrass does not produce viable seed so it must be planted by sprigs or sod. Because of its dense growth,

ST. AUGUSTINEGRASS CULTURE

■ Plant 3- to 4-inch sod plugs at 1-foot intervals any time during the growing season, as long as you can provide adequate water. During slow growth in spring and fall, keep the lawn free of weeds while it becomes established.
■ Mow regularly at 1–3 inches.
■ Fertilize frequently with up to 3–6 pounds of nitrogen per 1,000 square feet per year. Applications of ferrous sulfate or chelated iron will enhance the appearance of St. Augustinegrass and help prevent chlorosis or yellowing of the leaves.

PROS AND CONS

St. Augustinegrass forms a thick turf that crowds out weeds, stands up to wear and tolerates shade, heat, salty soil, and moderate cold. New varieties are more cold tolerant and tend to hold their green color longer than bermudagrass.

St. Augustinegrass requires high fertilizer levels and regular watering, and its subsequent rapid growth often leads to a build-up of thatch, which must be removed regularly. Even under the best conditions, it forms a coarse, rough-looking lawn.

St. Augustinegrass forms a springy turf that is prone to thatch, which must be removed regularly to allow moisture and fertilizer to penetrate the soil.

ST. AUGUSTINEGRASS AND CENTIPEDEGRASS CULTIVARS

ST. AUGUSTINEGRASS
'DelMar': excellent cold tolerance; good resistance to SAD virus and gray leaf spot; good shade tolerance.
'Floralawn': blue-green color; resistant to chinch bugs in some locations.
'FX-10': blue-gray color; good drought resistance; moderately resistant to chinch bugs.
'Jade': very good turf performance; good cold tolerance.

'Sunclipse': good turf performance; especially well adapted to climate in Southern California.

CENTIPEDEGRASS:
'Au-Centennial': semidwarf growth makes dense, low-growing sod.
'Oklawn': the first improved variety; superior drought and cold tolerance.

Lawn grasses rarely come in a bag as a single species; instead, they're sold as mixtures and blends (see page 61). When buying seed, check the label to see whether the bag contains these or other improved cultivars.

CENTIPEDEGRASS

Centipedegrass (*Eremochloa ophiuroides*), a coarse-textured, light green grass that spreads by way of leafy stolons, is sometimes called "lazy man's grass" because of its low maintenance requirements. It needs less mowing than other grasses, and it adapts to poor soil, resists chinch bugs and brown patch disease, and is aggressive enough to crowd out weeds. These qualities make it an excellent choice for general-purpose lawns in the Southeast and Gulf Coast states.

Centipedegrass has some drawbacks, however. Its shallow roots give it only moderate drought tolerance, and it is among the first of the warm-season grasses to turn brown during extended hot, dry periods.

Also sensitive to low temperatures, centipedegrass tends to go dormant when cold. It turns green again when temperatures warm up. However, extended periods of temperatures below 5° F can kill centipedegrass. It will not withstand much traffic and is slow to recover when damaged.

Centipedegrass should not be planted near beach areas because it cannot tolerate salt spray. It is particularly sensitive to iron deficiencies that can arise in alkaline soils.

CENTIPEDEGRASS CULTURE

■ Sow common centipedegrass seed at a rate of 1–2 pounds per 1,000 square feet. Plant sprigs or sod plugs of other varieties on 1-foot centers. Water thoroughly when centipedegrass shows signs of stress: wilted and discolored leaves. Apply iron sulfate if chlorosis appears.
■ Mow at 1–2 inches.
■ Fertilize with 2 pounds of nitrogen per 1,000 square feet per year on heavy soils, or 2–3 pounds of nitrogen on sandy soils.

PROS AND CONS

Centipedegrass is a relatively fine-bladed, dense growing turfgrass that thrives in sandy, acidic soils and requires low fertility. It grows slowly so it needs less frequent mowing than bermudagrass. However, the plant is susceptible to hard freezes. It is not salt tolerant and may require applications of iron. Even under the best conditions, centipedegrass does not tolerate heavy wear.

Centipedegrass

Blade: Flat; boat-shaped tip.
Ligule: Clear, purplish.
Collar: Hairy, cinched.
New leaf: Folded.

CARPETGRASS

Carpetgrass (*Axonopus fissifolius*) is a specialized creeping grass that forms a dense, fast-growing, wear-tolerant turf that grows well in the lower coastal plains of the United States.

It does not make an especially attractive lawn. Its blades are quite coarse, and the plant forms unattractive seed heads if allowed to grow more than an inch tall. Frequent mowing is a must to keep it below that height. However, if well maintained, carpetgrass is a disease- and insect-tolerant turfgrass that stands up to heavy wear.

This grass grows vigorously in sandy, acidic soils, even without additional fertilization. However, drought tolerance is not one of its strengths. In areas with infrequent rainfall, it must be irrigated regularly.

Carpetgrass is also cold sensitive and cannot survive winter temperatures north of central Georgia. Even in the Deep South, it will go dormant and turn brown during the relatively cooler winter months.

Native to the Gulf Coast, it grows best from Texas to Florida and north to Virginia. In those areas, it can withstand more shade and moisture than bermudagrass.

CARPETGRASS CULTURE

■ Sow 5–10 pounds of seed per 1,000 square feet, or plant sprigs 6–12 inches apart in rows 12 inches apart.
■ Mow every 10–14 days at 1–2 inches.
■ Fertilize with 1–3 pounds of nitrogen per 1,000 square feet per year.

PROS AND CONS

Carpetgrass grows vigorously by creeping stolons to form a dense, wear-tolerant turf that withstands low fertility. However, it has poor drought and cold tolerance. The grass is not attractive: It is light green, coarse textured and prone to forming seed heads. There are no improved cultivars of carpetgrass

Carpetgrass

Blade: Smooth; sharp tip.
Ligule: Long hairs.
Collar: Narrow, smooth.
New leaf: Folded.

GRASSES FOR TROUBLE SPOTS

You can grow a good-looking, trouble-free lawn in moderate shade if you choose the proper species and variety.

If your lawn seems to be struggling, you might be trying to grow the wrong grass. Maintaining a lawn is easy in good soil in the sun, but most of us are not so blessed. Fortunately, however, there are many turf grass species that thrive even in troublesome areas. The key to lawn success is finding the species that matches your conditions.

SHADY

Many grasses tolerate some degree of shade, but the best also withstand high mowing, which makes more blade surface available for photosynthesis in low light situations. If your lawn is shaded, look for a good drought-tolerant grass because shade is often caused by trees that compete for soil moisture. Good grasses for shade include the following:
COOL SEASON: rough bluegrass, fine fescue, tall fescue.
WARM SEASON: St. Augustinegrass, centipedegrass, bahiagrass.

DRY

The best drought-tolerant grasses usually are the ones that grow long roots to tap into all available soil moisture. The following are the most drought-tolerant species:
COOL SEASON: tall fescue, fine fescue.
WARM SEASON: bermudagrass (both common and hybrid), zoysiagrass, bahiagrass, buffalograss.

HOW GRASSES MEASURE UP

Grasses	Establishment Speed	Heat Tolerance	Cold Tolerance	Drought Tolerance	Shade Tolerance	Wearability	Low Mowing	Fertilizer Needs
COOL-SEASON GRASSES								
Creeping bentgrass	moderate	poor	good	poor	moderate	poor	good	high
Kentucky bluegrass	poor	moderate	good	moderate	moderate	moderate	moderate	moderate
Rough bluegrass	moderate	poor	good	poor	good	moderate	moderate	moderate
Canada bluegrass	poor	poor	good	moderate	moderate	poor	poor	low
Fine fescues	moderate	moderate	good	moderate	good	good	poor	moderate
Perennial ryegrass	good	moderate	moderate	moderate	moderate	good	moderate	moderate
Tall fescues	good	good	poor	good	moderate	good	poor	moderate
WARM-SEASON GRASSES								
Bahiagrass	moderate	good	poor	moderate	moderate	good	poor	low
Hybrid bermudagrass	good	good	moderate	good	poor	good	good	moderate
Blue gramagrass	moderate	good	moderate	good	poor	poor	moderate	low
Buffalograss	moderate	good	good	good	poor	moderate	good	good
Carpetgrass	moderate	high	poor	moderate	poor	poor	good	low
Centipedegrass	moderate	good	poor	moderate	moderate	poor	moderate	moderate
St. Augustinegrass	moderate	good	poor	poor	good	moderate	poor	moderate
Zoysiagrass	poor	good	moderate	good	moderate	good	good	low

HOT

Heat tolerance is relative. Warm-season grasses can, of course, take the heat better than cool-season varieties. Some of them often jump the bluegrass line into the hottest areas of cooler climates. Some cool-season grasses, on the other hand, show moderate and even good heat tolerance and can be planted in cooler areas of the South. The best turfgrasses for hot regions include:
COOL SEASON: perennial ryegrass, tall fescue, fine fescue, Kentucky bluegrass.
WARM SEASON: bermudagrasses, centipedegrass, zoysiagrass, St. Augustinegrass, buffalograss.

COLD

Most cool-season grasses survive even the severest winters, except those in the far North. Some, however, bounce back more quickly from the cold. Warm-season grasses vary tremendously in their ability to withstand cool temperatures even in the South. In some cases, cool-season grasses are substituted for warm-season grasses in the coolest areas of the warm-season zone. The best cold-tolerant grasses are:
COOL SEASON: fine fescue, creeping bentgrass, Canada and Kentucky bluegrasses
WARM SEASON: bermudagrasses, zoysiagrass, hybrid St. Augustinegrass

SLOPES

Grasses for lawns on slopes need to tolerate infrequent mowing, little to no fertilization and dry soil (slopes dry out faster than flat ground). These include:
COOL SEASON: hard fescue, sheep fescue
WARM SEASON: buffalograss, blue gramagrass

TRAFFIC

For heavily-used areas, grasses should have good vigor and strong crowns that can produce blades, even under constant traffic. Some examples:
COOL SEASON: tall fescue, perennial ryegrass, Kentucky bluegrass
WARM SEASON: bermudagrasses, bahiagrass, zoysiagrass

ADVANCES IN GRASSES

Turfgrass breeding has made a quantum leap in the second half of the 20th century. Before then, there were only a handful of commonly used turfgrass varieties, and most of them had serious shortcomings. They were often coarse-textured, light-colored, and had no resistance to insects or diseases. For the most part, they came straight from the pasture and had not been improved substantially for hundreds of years.

Things have changed with a dizzying speed. In 1960, there were six Kentucky bluegrass varieties. Now there are more than 70. There was one perennial ryegrass variety in 1960. By 1995 there were 107 of them. In 1960 there were two pale and weedy-looking tall fescues. Now there are at least 100, and they look almost as good as Kentucky bluegrass.

Across the board, grass blades have become finer and greener and the plants are tougher and more dense. Perhaps most significantly, breeders have imbued grasses with resistance to virtually every lawn disease known to man. And now, thanks to endophytes—microscopic fungi that are bred into grass varieties—many of them have resistance to insects as well.

Where do these new varieties come from? It starts with selection. Breeders scour the countryside for plants that exhibit outstanding characteristics: better color, vigor, drought tolerance. Then they take them back to trial grounds, and put them to the test. There they may be crossed with other improved plants to create hybrids, or simply grown out and re-selected.

Trial varieties may take 10 to 15 years to reach the market, but as they gradually appear on garden center shelves, they improve the appearance and performance of lawns across the country.

In university and seed company trials, hundreds of turfgrass varieties grow side-by-side in small plots to highlight differences in color, height, disease and insect resistance, and drought tolerance.

LOW MAINTENANCE

■ Mow regularly at the maximum height recommended for your grass species.
■ Fertilize annually with a slow-release fertilizer.
■ Water only when grass is severely stressed by drought.

MODERATE MAINTENANCE

■ Mow at least once a week.
■ Water twice a month, depending on rainfall.
■ Fertilize twice annually in the North, three times in the South.
■ Spot weed to prevent pernicious regrowth.
■ Aerate biannually.

INTENSIVE MAINTENANCE

■ Mow weekly to semiweekly.
■ Water regularly, depending on rainfall.
■ Fertilize monthly during the growing season.
■ Use pesticides to eradicate or prevent weeds, disease and insects.
■ Aerate annually.

LAWN CARE

What do you want from your lawn? Before you start weeding, feeding, and mowing, that's the question you need to answer. Do you want a lawn that stays green most of the summer and covers the ground well, even if some of that cover consists of weeds? Or do you want a neat, trim lawn with soft grass that's a pleasure to play on? Or is it the showcase lawn you desire, one that's the envy of the neighbors?

It's up to you. When it comes to lawns, what you see is what you give—in terms of time, money and dedication. There are innumerable levels of care for your lawn, but for the sake of simplicity, here's an overview of the three most common.

LOW MAINTENANCE

With a low-maintenance lawn, you'll sacrifice appearance for the work you save. It will have its fair share of weeds. There will probably be some bare or thin patches of turf, and your grass may turn yellow or brown during dry weather. In general, its overall appearance may be a bit shaggy. To keep a lawn from completely going downhill, you need to supply at least this much maintenance:

MOWING: At the very least, a lawn needs careful mowing on a regular basis at the prescribed height for the type of grass you're growing. You shouldn't mow so infrequently that the plant is shocked by losing too much leaf at one time.

WATERING: Where rainfall is sparse, deep watering may be required every week or two. However, in many regions the lawn may not need additional water. Even if weather turns dry, you can allow the lawn to go dormant.

FERTILIZING: A lawn needs minimal fertilization: one application in the fall in the North, one in spring and another in fall in the South. The actual amount of nitrogen you apply depends on the species, but it will most likely be only 1 to 3 pounds per 1,000 square feet per year. Using a mulching mower helps, too. The clippings add nitrogen to the soil as they break down.

MODERATE MAINTENANCE

A lawn maintained at a moderate level needs more frequent care—you may spend twice as much time tending it. You'll still find some

weeds in a moderately maintained lawn, though they won't be as visible as they would with a low-maintenance regime. Your grass should be thick and lush. Although your work and watering will prevent the lawn from browning out, it may not be a bright eye-catching green all season.

MOWING: Mow at least weekly at the top of the height range for the species. You may need to mow twice weekly during peak growth.

WATERING: Water enough to prevent dormancy from setting in. That may mean watering weekly during the hottest months.

FERTILIZING: Make one additional fertilization, in spring in the North and midsummer in the South. Mulched grass clippings will improve nitrogen content.

WEEDING: Control weeds with herbicides or by pulling or digging them. In time, however, moderately maintained turf should crowd out weeds. Aerate every two years or so to penetrate thatch and open up compacted soil to let air and water freely enter.

INTENSIVE MAINTENANCE

This is the regime for an award-winning lawn. Consistency of care is especially important at this level.

MOWING: Set the mower at the short end of the height range for the grass. Mow frequently during the peak growing season.

WATERING AND FERTILIZING: Provide 1 to 2 inches of water per week throughout the growing season and fertilize regularly.

CONTROLLING PESTS: Intensive maintenance means regular applications of pesticides. Be aware that intensively maintained lawns are sometimes more prone to problems from insects and disease than lawns under other regimes because the grass is succulent from all the good care. These lawns are also more likely to develop thatch.

No matter how you intend to maintain your lawn, the prescription is the same when starting from scratch: Improve soil tilth, organic matter content, and fertility to avoid long-term problems, and don't scrimp on seed. A cheap variety will result in nothing but headaches later. Take time to shop around for an improved variety with resistance to disease and the ability to stand up to the conditions prevalent in your yard. The result will be a bright green, weed-free lawn.

LAWN CHECKUP

The first step in launching a good lawn-care program is to take stock of the lawn's condition as well as the state of its site. Check your lawn at least three times during the growing season: in spring and again in summer and fall.

Also, keep a journal for your lawn as you would for other plantings. Use the journal to keep track of lawn checkups, along with a record of routine maintenance. Note when you feed, water, and mow, and the lawn's response, as well as any problems such as diseases and insects that occur. If possible, keep track of when they first appear, weather conditions at that time and recent cultural activities.

Keep your lawn journal up-to-date. In time, you will see patterns emerge, and you'll be able to prevent problems before they occur.

LAND: Start your checkup by mapping out the general lay of the land. Make note of slopes, wet spots, shady areas, and dead-air pockets caused by buildings and trees. Look for dry spots around driveways and sidewalks where snow, ice, or water pile up during the winter.

TESTING SOIL TEXTURE

There are a couple of ways to get a rough idea of the texture of your soil. For the first test, take several teaspoon-size samples from the top 6 inches of the soil at several locations in your lawn. Let the samples dry thoroughly, then pulverize them with a rolling pin.

Fill a quart jar two-thirds full of water, stir in 1 teaspoon of dishwasher detergent, add the soil, cover, and shake vigorously. Over time the soil will separate out into layers of sand, silt, and clay.

The sand particles will quickly settle to the bottom of the jar. With a grease pencil, mark their level on the side of the jar. After two hours, the silt will settle into a layer on top of the sand. Mark the top of this layer. Finally, let the jar sit for two weeks; by that time the clay may have settled out and the remaining water will be clear. Mark the top of the clay level.

After you've made all the marks, you can estimate the relative amount of each soil type in your soil. If one type is more than one-half the total amount, that is your dominant soil texture.

The ribbon test is faster but not as precise. Moisten a handful of soil, then roll it between your open palms to form a ribbon or rope. If the soil feels gritty and refuses to hold a shape, it's mostly sand. If it feels smooth and silky and holds a ribbon shape briefly before breaking apart, it's high in silt. If, on the other hand, it feels sticky and holds together in a ribbon or rope shape, it's mostly clay.

GRASS: Then observe the condition of the grass, especially grass growing in heavy traffic areas. Is it vigorous or lagging? Is it rich-green or yellowish-brown? Does it have brown patches or other indications of disease?

How many different grass species or varieties are growing in your lawn? In the South, it's probably one, but in the North there could be several. They may be well integrated, but you may find patches of one growing where it has found its favorite site.

The box on page 29, along with the descriptions and photos in the grass gallery, will help you determine which species are present. Then to save time, energy, and money, get to know the cultural requirements of each grass you're growing. Grasses vary considerably in their need for water, fertilizer, mowing, and other cultural practices.

Roughly estimate the weed population by stretching a rope across the yard, then walk along it counting the number of times your foot lands on a weed.

SOIL: Test the soil every few years to determine its fertility. You can order a kit from the local cooperative extension office or a private soil testing service. Follow the directions for taking the test on page 58, and within a few weeks, the lab will send you a report, detailing the soil's nutrient levels, its pH and recommendations for improvement.

Lawns growing in clay soils often need frequent aeration. In sandy soil, they need extra water. The box at left will help you determine your soil type and set up a lawn-care schedule to match.

WEEDS: Weeds are an inevitable problem in any lawn. Up to a point, the damage threshold is determined by aesthetics. But if your lawn consists of more than 50 percent weeds, you're fighting a losing battle. To find out just how weedy your lawn is, do a quick weed check. Diagonally stretch a rope or hose across the lawn, and with pen and paper in hand, walk along it, marking each time your foot touches a weed. Then divide the number of steps that touched a weed by the total number of steps you took walking across the lawn for a rough percentage of weeds in the lawn.

INSECTS: Insects can usually be managed fairly easily, but first you have to recognize the signs of their damage. Look for chewed blades, damaged crowns, patches of brown and loose sod. To check for crown-dwelling pests, such as chinch bugs, cut both ends off a 2-pound coffee can and jam it a few inches into the soil. Fill the can with water and watch for insects to float to the top. See the section on insects (beginning on page 76) for more information on scouting for insect pests.

DISEASES: Check for symptoms of disease: brown circles, discolored blades, grass dying in patches. Note how long it takes the damage to spread, whether it disappears on its own, and how fast the grass recovers. Keep track of whether these symptoms occur in response to a climactic stress or a cultural practice.

Remove both ends from a 2-pound coffee can and jam it into the ground. Fill it with water, then count the number of insects that float to the top.

GRASS DETECTIVE

From a distance, all grasses look pretty much the same, but upon close inspection many show different characteristics. Those differences can help you identify the grass, then pursue a cultural regime to suit it.

Note the color of the grass. Is it a deep, rich green or yellowish? Keep track of its active growth period. Does it grow most vigorously in cool or warm weather?

Is it a creeping or a bunch grass? Dig up a plant and note how it spreads. Does it have rhizomes or stolons? Measure the width of the blades. Check to see if they're smooth or saw-like.

Now take a closer look. Examine the various parts of the grass plant. Note the shape of the blade. Is the tip boat-shaped or pointed? Take a close look at the sheath—the wrapping that encloses the stem. Note its color and whether it's split or smooth. Then find the ligule, the thin membrane or ring of hairs inside the leaf at the collar. Is it long or short? Using all of these clues, refer to the diagrams and text in the grass gallery to make an identification.

Cut a patch of sod and carefully roll it back. If you find more than five grubs, it's time to take action.

FERTILIZING

Like any other plant, turfgrass needs nutrients to survive. Because grasses compete with one another and with other plants and because mowing removes a good portion of their photosynthesizing surface, they can become nutrient deficient.

Grass plants require 16 chemical elements essential for growth. Three—carbon, hydrogen, and oxygen—are readily available from air and water. The rest must come from soil or fertilizer.

Nitrogen, phosphorus, and potassium are known as primary nutrients because plants use them in the greatest quantities. Nitrogen is by

Nitrogen provides the fuel that keeps grasses green and growing vigorously. If the grass grows slowly and is pale green or yellowish like the plants on the right, it may be a sign of nitrogen deficiency in the soil.

NUTRIENT VALUE OF CLIPPINGS

If you bag and dispose of your lawn clippings, you're throwing away a valuable resource. Lawn clippings are high in nutrients that can be returned to the soil. In fact, researchers at the University of Connecticut Agricultural Station found that over the course of a season, the clippings from a 1,000-square-foot area contribute nearly 2 pounds of nitrogen. The amount of nitrogen released depends on how much you fertilize, but even from a low-maintenance lawn, grass clippings from 1,000 square feet can provide ½ pound of nitrogen a season.

Those clippings decompose faster than you might think. And, no, they don't contribute to thatch buildup. Clippings begin to break down almost as soon as they hit the ground. Within a week, nitrogen released from them begins to show up in new growth.

far the most important element for a lawn. It promotes rapid shoot growth and gives lawns a healthy color. Because some forms of nitrogen leach from the soil and it is the element used in the largest amounts, most fertilizer recommendations for lawns are based on the amount of nitrogen to apply.

Turfgrass has less need for phosphorus than nitrogen, but phosphorus still is essential for healthy growth. It stimulates early formation and strong growth of roots. Soil usually contains enough phosphorus for established lawns, but "starter fertilizers," which are higher in phosphorus, can help new lawns.

Potassium strengthens lawn grasses, helping them to withstand traffic, resist diseases and conserve water. Like nitrogen, potassium is leached out of the soil, but at a slower rate.

Most commercial lawn fertilizers are heavy on nitrogen, and light on the other two elements, 32-2-3 and 28-3-4, for example. The numbers represent the percentage of nitrogen, phosphorus, and potassium, respectively, in a bag of fertilizer.

The secondary nutrients—calcium, magnesium, and sulfur—are nutrients turfgrasses require in relatively high amounts but not as much as the primary nutrients. These nutrients facilitate nitrogen uptake by the plant and increase root growth. If calcium is not present in adequate levels in the soil, add it with periodic applications of lime. Dolomitic limestone will supply magnesium as well as calcium. Lawns don't normally require

Phosphorus helps turfgrasses get off to a good start by encouraging root formation. You can pick out the phosphorus-deficient plots in this photo from their dark cast.

Rainfall and irrigation dissolve the nutrients in fertilizer and move them into the soil. Once there, soil microorganisms break down the fertilizer into a form that's available to plants. Plants then take up the nutrients through their roots and translocate them through the plant's vascular system to the leaves (red lines). The plant then uses these nutrients, along with energy from the sun, to create carbohydrates, which it stores in its roots, stolons, rhizomes, and crown (yellow lines). Liquid fertilizers work a little differently—when applied, plants absorb some of the nutrients directly through their leaves.

How much fertilizer you need to apply, as well as how frequently you need to apply it depends on the type of grass growing in your yard, the type of soil, and the maintenance regime you have selected.

sulfur, but if necessary, add it in the form of elemental sulfur or gypsum (calcium sulfate).

Even though plants use only tiny quantities of micronutrients, such as iron, manganese, zinc, and boron, they are as essential for growth as primary and secondary nutrients. However, apply them only when a soil test indicates a deficiency. Micronutrients can be toxic to the plants at low levels.

The micronutrient most often lacking in lawns is iron, especially in alkaline soils. If your lawn doesn't become greener with an application of nitrogen, it may need iron.

HOW MUCH FERTILIZER?

Each grass has an optimum fertility range, as outlined in the Nitrogen Needs of Grasses on page 35. However, several factors come into play in terms of which nutrients and how much of them you will need to supply.

For example, watering leaches nitrogen out of the soil and makes the lawn grow fast. So if you water, your lawn will need nitrogen. Sandy soils tend to be infertile, and they readily leach nutrients; clay is just the opposite. Lawns growing on sandy soil need more fertilizer than on clay. Leaving clippings returns nutrients to the lawn, as much as 30 percent of the total required.

Turfgrasses are especially vulnerable to a deficiency of iron in the soil. When iron is lacking, the grass will not turn a healthy green, no matter how much nitrogen you apply.

FERTILIZERS

Shopping for fertilizers can be a confusing chore. The elements in them, especially nitrogen, come in many forms, not to mention formulations and brands. To help make your shopping a little easier, here is a look at the general classes of lawn fertilizers.

SOLUBLE SYNTHETIC FERTILIZERS

The most common and least expensive fertilizers are soluble synthetics. These are concentrated fertilizers produced from a chemical reaction using organic or inorganic raw materials. Included in this group of fertilizers are ammonium nitrate, ammonium sulfate, and urea.

Soluble synthetics readily dissolve in water, and so are often called quick-release fertilizers. Their advantages are speed and predictability. Grass quickly greens up after application, and because soluble synthetics don't depend on microbial action to release nutrients, they are effective when soil is cold.

Composted sewage sludge, an organic fertilizer

Soluble synthetics have several disadvantages, however. Their effects are short-lived, so you must apply them several times in a growing season. Grass grows rapidly after application, requiring frequent mowing, then goes through a slump as the fertilizer runs out. In rainy periods or in well-watered areas, the nitrogen can leach through the soil beyond root reach. Also, the properties that allow soluble synthetics to dissolve in water also allow them to pull water out of plants, which can result in fertilizer burn.

To minimize these problems, many manufacturers combine soluble synthetics with the next category of fertilizers: slow-release fertilizers.

Inorganic water-soluble fertilizer

SLOW-RELEASE FERTILIZERS

Also called controlled-release, and timed-release fertilizers, slow-release fertilizers provide nutrients at a predictable rate. They ensure uniform turf growth throughout the season. You can apply them heavily without fear of burning the lawn. However they do not provide as quick a greenup and may be expensive to use.

One category of slow-release fertilizer has the nitrogen bound in a complex molecular compound. Until the compound breaks down, the nitrogen is unavailable to plants. Ureaformaldehyde (UF for short), is the most common of this group. Because UF is broken down by microbes, nutrients are available to plants only when soil is warm enough for microbial activity.

Other slow-release fertilizers contain what is known as water-insoluble nitrogen. There are several types of water-insoluble nitrogen, including IBDU (isobutyline diurea) and methylene urea.

IBDU releases nutrients most efficiently when soil temperatures are above 75° F. It supplies nitrogen for about 60 days. Methylene urea releases nitrogen through bacterial activity and so is dependent on soil temperature and moisture. It can be formulated to last the entire growing season.

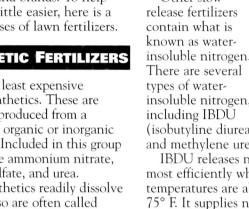

Granular form of synthetic lawn fertilizer

The last group of slow-release fertilizers are the coated fertilizers. With these, individual particles of quick-release nitrogen are covered with a material that lets out only small amounts of nutrients at a time, usually only when the fertilizer is wet. Some manufacturers coat the particles with a semipermeable resin or plastic-like material and can program the fertilizer to release nutrients for a specified period lasting three to six months. Other coated fertilizers are a mix of pellets having coatings of varying thicknesses, which release the fertilizer at different rates. Sulfur-coated urea (also called SCU) is the most common of these.

NATURAL ORGANIC FERTILIZERS

The term natural organic refers to any fertilizer that is made up of dried or composted plant or animal waste. A wide variety of natural organic fertilizers are on the market. Among the ones most suitable for use on turf are those made from sewage sludge and poultry waste.

Blended fertilizer containing a mix of materials

Organic fertilizers offer many benefits. Most have soil-building properties, improving soil structure and organic matter content in addition to providing nutrients. The nitrogen

READING A FERTILIZER LABEL

By law, all fertilizer labels must include the same basic information:

The three large numbers are the analysis of the fertilizer. They indicate the percentages of nitrogen, phosphorus, and potassium, in that order, making up the contents of the fertilizer package. In this product, the nutrients are combined in a ratio of 10 to 1 to 1.

Guaranteed analysis is the manufacturer's warranty that the stated analysis by weight is true.

PREMIUM

Lawn Fertilizer

30-3-3

GUARANTEED ANALYSIS

Total Nitrogen (N)...30.0%
　4.9% Ammoniacal Nitrogen
　15.1% Urea Nitrogen
　9.2% Water-soluble Organic Nitrogen
　0.8% Water-insoluble Nitrogen
Available Phosphate (P₂O₅)............................3.0%
Soluble Potash (K₂O).....................................3.0%
Sulfur (S) Total................................3.0%
Iron (Fe)...........................1.7%
Derived from: Monoammonium Phosphate, Urea, Methylene Ureas, Sulfate of Potash, Ammonium Sulfate, Iron Sulfate
*Contains 7.5% slowly available methylenediurea and dimethylenetriurea nitrogen.

KEEP OUT OF REACH OF CHILDREN

Though not required by law, most manufacturers also list the various forms of nitrogen in the package, including the percentage of water-soluble and water-insoluble nitrogen. Because this product is mostly ammonium and urea, it is a fast-acting fertilizer. However, the addition of water-insoluble and water-soluble-organic nitrogen means the product lasts longer than if it contained fast-release nitrogen alone.

All secondary and micronutrients in the fertilizer are also listed on the label by percentage.

The sources of the primary and secondary nutrients in the fertilizer package are listed after the guaranteed analysis.

---

contained in natural organic fertilizers is usually water insoluble. Until soil microbes break them down, these fertilizers don't release their nitrogen. That means they release nutrients slowly, providing plants with a steady supply of "food" through the growing season. Thus, there's little danger of overfertilizing with organic fertilizers or of excess nitrogen leaching through the soil. Organic fertilizers also often contain valuable micronutrients.

On the negative side: Compared to synthetic fertilizers, organics generally contain a lower percentage of nitrogen per pound so you'll need to apply them in much greater amounts to achieve the same effect as synthetic fertilizers provide. That increases the cost to fertilize. And, because natural organics depend on soil microorganisms for the release of nutrients, they are weather dependent. They will "work" only if the temperature is above 50° F.

COMPARING FERTILIZER COSTS

Finding the best buy in a mountain of fertilizer bags at the garden center can be a daunting task. With their different volumes, analyses, and ingredients, it feels like comparing apples to oranges. But you can find a common denominator for comparison by doing a little math to determine the cost per pound of actual nitrogen.

Suppose you're trying to choose between a 40-pound bag of 34-0-0 that sells for $10.98, and a 40-pound bag of 21-5-7 for $7.50. Which offers you the most nitrogen bang for the buck?

Here's how to decide:

First, convert the nitrogen in the bag to a percentage by multiplying it by 0.01. (Nitrogen is the first in the three-number analysis for the fertilizer. In 21-5-7, 21 is the nitrogen.) Here, 34 x 0.01 = 0.34; 21 x 0.01 = 0.21.

Next, multiply the total pounds of fertilizer in the bag by the percentage of nitrogen to determine how many pounds of actual nitrogen are in the bag. (40 x 0.34 = 13.6 pounds of actual nitrogen in the first bag; 40 x 0.21 = 8.4 pounds of actual nitrogen in the second.)

Finally, divide the cost of the bag by the pounds of actual nitrogen to determine cost per pound of nitrogen ($10.98 / 13.6 = $.81 per pound of actual nitrogen; $7.50 / 8.4 = $.89 per pound of actual nitrogen).

In this example, the bag of 34-0-0 offers a slightly better value in terms of cost of nitrogen. However, this product doesn't contain phosphorus and potassium, as the 21-5-7 does.

FEEDING TIME

It's best to fertilize lawns when they begin their active growth period: spring and summer for warm-season grasses; spring and fall for cool-season grasses.

"When should I fertilize the lawn?" It seems like a simple question, one that should warrant a straightforward answer, but nothing in lawn care evokes more confusion and disagreement than fertilizer schedules. Some say spring is the best time to fertilize; others recommend autumn. Some advocate both spring and fall feeding, while still others will advise you to fertilize every month of the growing season. Who's right? All of them, and none of them. In fact, there's no one right schedule. The time to fertilize depends on many factors, including where you live, the species of grass you grow, and the kind of lawn you want.

However, there is one general rule that nearly everyone can follow. It is best to fertilize your lawn when it begins its active growth period. This is usually (but not always) spring and fall for cool-season grasses. For warm-season grasses, it's late spring—after the grass breaks dormancy—through summer. If you fertilize at the beginning of these seasons, your lawn will have full benefit of the nutrients during the entire time it is growing.

However, there is one exception to this general rule. Late spring is not the best time to fertilize cool-season grasses with a quick-release fertilizer. At this time, quick-release fertilizer encourages lush growth that may not be able to withstand summer heat. However, applying a slow-release fertilizer at this time helps the grass survive the stresses of summer.

Fall fertilization keeps cool-season grasses growing longer into cold weather, stimulating the lawn to thicken. As the grass slows its growth in fall, it will store carbohydrates to help it survive winter and to use to get off to a fast start the next spring. Fall feeding provides the nutrients cool-season grasses need to form the carbohydrates.

Warm-season grasses are a different story. Their growth peaks in midsummer, then tapers off in fall, continuing at a slower pace until frost. Late spring and summer are the best times for fertilizing warm-season turfgrasses. Make the first application when the grass first starts to green up in spring, using quick-acting forms of nitrogen.

Summer feeding keeps the lawn going through the hot season, but be careful about fertilizing in late summer or fall. That may promote a flush of succulent growth that leaves the grass more susceptible to injury when cold weather arrives.

How often you fertilize during these feeding periods depends on your choice of a maintenance regime. For low-maintenance lawns in the North, fertilize once in fall. In the South, fertilize once after spring greenup and again in early summer. For medium-maintenance, cool-season lawns, fertilize in late summer and fall, or in spring and fall. Fertilize warm-season lawns once in spring, once in midsummer, and once in fall. For high-maintenance lawns, whatever the type, fertilize monthly during active growth periods.

FERTILIZER WORKSHEET

To determine how much fertilizer to use per 1,000 square feet, complete the following calculations:

Pounds of actual nitrogen required per year per 1,000 square feet (from the chart at right),

DIVIDED BY:
Percentage of nitrogen in lawn fertilizer (the first number of the label),

EQUALS
Pounds of fertilizer required per year per 1,000 square feet.

FOR EXAMPLE
In a high-fertilizer regime, Kentucky bluegrass requires 3 pounds of actual nitrogen per year per 1,000 square feet.

A bag of 10-6-4 lawn fertilizer contains 10 percent actual nitrogen. And 3 divided by 0.10 (10 percent converted to a decimal) equals 30. So 1,000 square feet of Kentucky bluegrass would require 30 pounds of 10-6-4 fertilizer per year.

NITROGEN NEEDS OF GRASSES

The chart below lists the actual nitrogen requirements for various species of grasses. (The first analysis number on a bag of fertilizer represents the percentage of nitrogen in the fertilizer.) The numbers represent the range of nitrogen needed from minimum to maximum. Use the first number for a low-maintenance lawn and the higher number for a high-maintenance lawn. If your lawn contains a mixture of two or more grasses, use the average of their requirements. In areas with high rainfall, a long growing season, or sandy soil, you should adjust the requirements upward slightly. Leaving grass clippings on the lawn will reduce them slightly.

Grass	Pounds of Actual Nitrogen Per Year
COOL SEASON GRASSES	
Bentgrasses	2–6
Chewings fescue	1–2
Hard fescue	1–2
Red fescue	1–2
Sheep fescue	1–2
Tall fescue	1–2
Kentucky bluegrass	2–3
Rough bluegrass	1–2
Canada bluegrass	2–3
Perennial ryegrass	2–3
Annual ryegrass	2–3
WARM SEASON GRASSES	
Bahiagrass	2–4
Bermudagrass	1–4
Blue gramagrass	1–2
Buffalograss	1–2
Carpetgrass	1–3
Centipedegrass	2–3
St. Augustinegrass	3–6
Zoysiagrass	2–3

HOW TO FERTILIZE

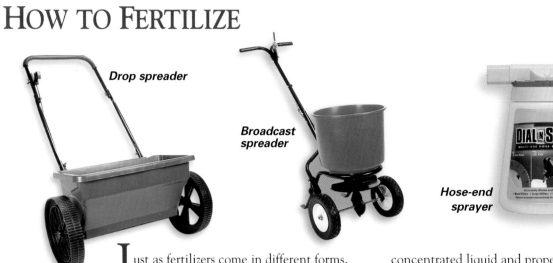

Drop spreader

Broadcast spreader

Hose-end sprayer

Just as fertilizers come in different forms, so do their methods of application. Apply liquid fertilizers with a hand-held hose-end sprayer. For dry fertilizers, use either a drop or a broadcast spreader, both of which you can purchase or rent from a nursery.

Always fill sprayers and spreaders over a sidewalk or driveway. If you happen to spill concentrated fertilizer on the lawn, hose it away or scrape or vacuum it up, then flood the area with water to avoid fertilizer burn.

HOSE-END SPRAYERS: This sprayer has a plastic or glass body suspended beneath a nozzle that attaches to a hose. Water flowing through the sprayer mixes with the concentrated liquid and propels it through the nozzle, spraying up to 15 gallons of fertilizer.

To use a hose-end sprayer, simply measure the fertilizer into the sprayer container and fill it with water to the proper level. Spray the entire contents of the sprayer onto your lawn, providing equal coverage to all sections.

The water and fertilizer mix together at a fixed rate. So always read the directions for both the sprayer and the fertilizer to determine how much fertilizer to measure into the container.

DROP SPREADERS: As the name implies, drop spreaders simply drop fertilizer from a bin. Their application is more precise than a broadcast spreader, but because they apply

CALIBRATING A SPREADER

Most drop and broadcast spreaders have adjustable settings, corresponding to the application rates on fertilizer bags. However, fertilizer labels often don't list all brands of spreaders, and some fertilizers, especially organic ones, do not come with calibration information. In that case you'll have to calibrate the spreader yourself to ensure you apply the fertilizer at the proper rate.

Here's how. If your spreader is equipped with a collection pan, measure its width, then attach it. Fill the spreader with fertilizer and operate it for a pre-measured distance, say 100 feet. Weigh the amount of fertilizer in the pan. (If your spreader doesn't have a collection pan,

run it over a smooth surface such as plastic or a clean concrete floor, then sweep up the fertilizer and weigh it.) Multiply the width of the spreader by the distance traveled to determine the area covered. The fertilization rate of your spreader equals the number of pounds in the collection pan for the area covered.

For example, a spreader with a 2-foot-wide drop travels 100 feet and delivers 1 pound of material. The area covered is 200 square feet. Your spreader at this calibration applies fertilizer at a rate of 1 pound per 200 square feet, or 5 pounds per 1,000 square feet (1,000 ÷ 200 = 5 x 1 pound = 5 pounds).

SPREADER PATTERNS

When applying fertilizer, a broadcast spreader is faster, but less precise than a drop spreader. It throws fertilizer over a wider area, but applies less fertilizer at the ends of its range. The best way to get uniform coverage with a broadcast spreader is to cover the ends of the lawn first, then go back and forth the long way. To avoid fertilizing

an area more than once, shut off the spreader as you approach the end of a strip.

When using a drop spreader, it's best to go back and forth across the lawn. Overlap the wheel tracks enough that no strips are left underfertilized, but also be careful not to double-feed any sections.

fertilizer to a narrower area, you have to make more passes. Drop spreaders are most useful on small- to medium-sized lawns.

When using a drop spreader, overlap your passes enough that no strips are left underfed, but also be careful not to double up on any sections. Missing sections will leave streaks in your lawn; doubling up can cause fertilizer burn.

BROADCAST SPREADERS: A broadcast spreader—either hand-held or push-wheel—is the easiest applicator to use for dry fertilizers. It throws the fertilizer granules or pellets over a wide area by means of a whirling wheel. The hand-held model operates through a side-arm crank. It is best for small lawns. Not only is it somewhat awkward to use, but it is also less accurate. The push-wheel model flings fertilizer from the bottom of a hopper as you push it across the lawn.

For either type, you need to know the width of the spreader's throw so you know how close to space your passes. You can easily determine throw width by filling the spreader with light-colored material, then running it over dark-colored pavement for a short distance. Usually, if you overlap passes by one-fourth their width, you can ensure uniform coverage and avoid streaks in the lawn.

The best technique for applying fertilizer with a broadcast spreader is to cover the ends of the lawn first, then go back and forth between the ends. To avoid double applications, shut off the spreader as you approach the end strips. Keep the spreader closed while turning, backing up,

or stopping. For even, thorough coverage, walk at a normal speed and keep the spreader level.

Because it requires fewer passes to completely cover the lawn, a broadcast spreader is easier to use than a drop spreader, especially on large lawns. Streaking is also less likely with broadcast spreaders because the swaths of fertilizer overlap and the edges of the swaths are less distinct than those produced by drop spreaders.

CALIBRATION

Both broadcast and drop spreaders have adjustable settings for use with different brands of fertilizer. Usually the spreaders come with a chart that tells you which setting to use for most brands of fertilizer, or the fertilizer has a chart on its bag. However, the openings in the spreader can wear out over time. It's a good idea to calibrate spreaders yearly to ensure they dispense fertilizer at the correct rate.

One calibration technique is to draw a 100-square-foot area on a level section of concrete, such as a driveway or patio. Sweep the area clean, fill the hopper with fertilizer, then spread the fertilizer in the marked area.

Sweep up the fertilizer and weigh it. This tells you how much fertilizer the spreader is putting out per 100 square feet. To find how much it will apply over 1,000 square feet, multiply the weight of the swept-up fertilizer by 10. If that doesn't match the amount you came up with using the Fertilizer Worksheet on page 35, try another setting and repeat.

WHY WE MOW

At some point, all of us have asked ourselves the question: What would happen if we didn't mow the lawn, if we just let it grow to its natural height? After all, it seems odd to spend so much effort and money getting the grass to grow, only to cut it back relentlessly.

So let's just imagine what would happen if we left the lawn unmown. The grass, of course, would grow upward and top out at 4 to 24 inches, depending on the species.

As it grew, it would begin the natural process of sexual reproduction. The grass would produce flowers—no, not gorgeous blooms, not even attractive ones. The flowers of a grass plant are green, like the leaves, and grow on stiff, wiry stems. And they're a major source of allergy-producing pollen.

After flowering, the plant would set seed, and then the seeds would ripen and fall. Wind and foot traffic would bend over and break leaf blades and flower stems, making the lawn appear abandoned and neglected.

In the meantime, the turf would thin out because the outward spread of the grass is slowed by not mowing. Mowing actually helps make the lawn grow thicker. You might say that because mown grass can't grow up, it grows out, but it's a bit more complicated than that.

The tip of each grass blade contains hormones that repress horizontal growth. Cutting off the tips with each mowing

SMART WAYS TO SAVE TIME SPENT ON MOWING

Maneuvering around trees consumes a lot of time while mowing the lawn. You can reduce the wasted time by surrounding trees with mulch to make mowing easier.

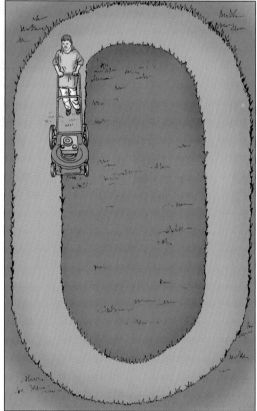

The more corners your lawn contains, the more time you'll waste mowing in and out of them. Design your lawn with soft, circular sides and no sharp edges and you'll save lots of time.

If your lawn does have corners, try this trick to save time. On your first mowing pass, round off the corners, leaving them unmown. After you've finished mowing the cornerless part of the lawn, go back and mow the corners. That way you only have to deal with the corners once, not on every pass around the lawn.

removes the hormones and allows the grass to spread outward more vigorously.

If you left the grass unmown then later decided to mow it, you would cut off the plants' growing points. The result would be an even thinner lawn that's thatchy because leaf and flower stems are what make up thatch.

All in all, if you let the lawn grow without mowing, using it would be much less pleasant. Not only would the wiry flower stems make sitting and playing on the lawn uncomfortable, the thinning turf would not cushion falls as well and would be less safe for children roughhousing on the lawn. Also, the long leaves would provide a good home for chiggers, snakes and other possibly undesirable animals.

Mowing offers other benefits. It obviously makes the lawn look better, keeping it neat and trim all year. In spring, mowing removes damaged and brown tips. Mowing also helps keep weed populations down by keeping the turf thick with no holes for weeds to invade.

One of the best ways to cut your mowing time is to use the largest mower that's practical for your lawn. Mowing a one-acre lawn with a 24-inch mower will save about an hour over mowing the same size lawn with an 18-inch-wide mower.

While trying to save time, don't be tempted to scrimp on mower coverage. When you mow, it's important to overlap each pass by at least three inches. That will ensure an even mowing with no skipped strips. One of the best ways to save time is to use a mower with a wide cutting bed.

However, to be honest, not every effect of mowing is positive. The very nature of mowing injures plants. The cut end is a site for pathogens to enter the grass plant. Every mowing is a bit of a shock to the plant, which forces it to put its energy into growing new leaves rather than roots. So the root systems of mowed grass tend to be less extensive than unmowed grass, and mowed plants store fewer carbohydrates.

This dual nature of mowing has a big influence on how healthy a lawn is. Although mowing is destructive, it is also positive, if done correctly. And that's the key. Improper mowing is one of the most common causes of turf problems. The following pages will help you to do it right.

MOWING RULES

When it comes to mowing, there's one axiom to observe. That's the rule of one-third. It says: Never remove more than one-third of the surface area of the grass blade at any one time.

Suppose, for example, you have a Kentucky bluegrass lawn with an ideal height of 2 inches. If you let it grow to 3 inches, but no higher, you can cut it back by 1 inch, and you've removed just one-third of the blade and restored the plant to its ideal height.

WHY ONE-THIRD?

If you let the grass grow too high, then cut it back by half or more, you shock the plant down to its roots. In fact, there is a direct relationship between mowing height and depth of roots. Mowed at its recommended height, grass roots grow deep. But if cut severely, root growth slows, and the grass is less vigorous and more subject to stress because its energy is directed to replacing lost leaves.

The grass will recover, but it may take several weeks. During this recovery period, the plant will need to tap into the carbohydrates it has stored to get through winter and stressful weather. So drought or excessive heat during or soon after this period can set the grass back even further.

Also, at low cutting heights, diseases such as dollar spot, leaf spot, and rust are more of a problem because they can envelop the whole plant more quickly.

An occasional too-low mowing is usually a temporary setback. But if you routinely cut off more than a third of the grass—either by setting the mowing height too low or sticking to a once-a-week schedule—you can expect your lawn to thin out, be weedy and subject to diseases and other problems.

If you return from vacation and are faced with an overgrown lawn, you should not try to mow it back to its preferred height immediately. Instead, mow lightly, removing one-third of the blade or less. Then allow the

SCALPED VS. CORRECT

One of the most common and costly lawn care mistakes is scalping the grass—cutting off more than one-third the height of the blade at any one time. Removing too much of the grass blade in any one mowing shocks the plant and dramatically slows the growth of the roots. It also exposes the shaded stems to too much sunlight, causing them to burn. On the other hand, cutting one-third or less of the blade allows the roots to continue growing deeply to strengthen the plant.

If the lawn has a yellowish or brownish cast immediately after mowing, that's a sure sign that it has been scalped.

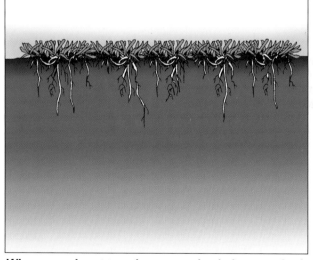

When grass is cut too short, or scalped, the growth of the roots is slowed, and plant growth is virtually halted until the leaves can recover.

When grass is properly mown, with less than one-third of the blade removed, the roots continue growing, and the grass thrives.

grass to recover for two or three days, and remove another one-third. Continue until the grass reaches the right height.

MOWING TIPS

Just how and when you mow depends on several factors including the type of grass, the season of the year, and the amount of fertilizer and water applied. For example, cool-season grasses need mowing more in spring and fall, warm-season grasses in summer. And the more you fertilize and water, the more you'll need to mow. The important element is flexibility. You may have to mow twice a week during peak growth periods or only twice a month during the slow times.

When you mow, vary your pattern. Mowing in the same direction every time tends to compact soil. Grass leans or grows in the direction it is mowed, so altering the mowing pattern will keep it straighter.

Do not cut wet grass. It mows unevenly, and the clippings clog the mower as well as mat on the grass, blocking light.

For safety's sake, mow slight slopes on a diagonal. If the ground is uneven, avoid scalping high spots. Either raise the mowing height or regrade the area.

MOWING HEIGHTS IN INCHES

Grass	Minimum Height	Maximum Height
COOL-SEASON GRASSES		
Bentgrasses	1/4	3/4
Chewings fescue	1 1/2	2 1/2
Hard fescue	1 1/2	2 1/2
Red fescue	1 1/2	2 1/2
Sheep fescue	2	4
Tall fescue	1 1/2	3
Kentucky bluegrass	1 1/2	2 1/2
Rough bluegrass	2	3
Canada bluegrass	3	4
Perennial ryegrass	1 1/2	2 1/2
Annual ryegrass	1 1/2	2 1/2
WARM-SEASON GRASSES		
Bahiagrass	2	3
Bermudagrass	1/2	1
Blue gramagrass	2	3
Buffalograss	2	3
Carpetgrass	1	2
Centipedegrass	1	2
St. Augustinegrass	1	3
Zoysiagrass	1/2	1

DEVELOPING A MOWING SCHEDULE FOR TURFGRASSES

Rather than basing a mowing schedule on the calendar, you should build your own schedule based on the needs of your lawn.

■ Determine the maximum and minimum mowing height for your grass, using the chart above.

■ As soon as the lawn greens up in spring, allow it to grow to its maximum mowing height, then cut it back to its minimum height, but do not remove more than one-third of its length at any one time.

■ When summer arrives, allow the grass to exceed the maximum height by about one-third, then cut it back to its maximum height, again removing no more than one-third.

■ Continue mowing at this height until fall, when the grass stops growing or goes dormant.

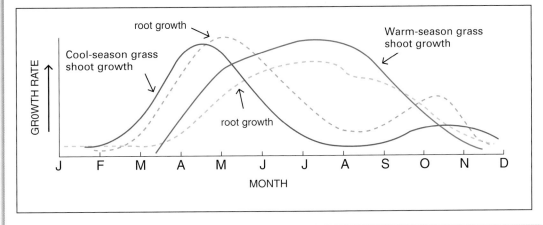

CHOOSING THE RIGHT MACHINE

We spend a lot of time behind our lawn mowers—an average of 40 hours per year—but we really don't know as much about them as we should. In fact, the mower we're steering across the lawn might not be the best one for the job.

There are two basic types of lawn mowers: rotary and reel. Each has its advantages and disadvantages.

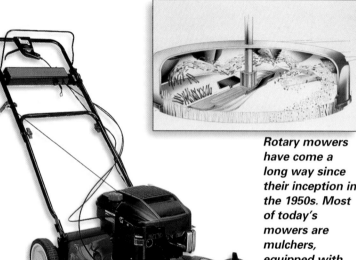

Rotary mowers have come a long way since their inception in the 1950s. Most of today's mowers are mulchers, equipped with blades that finely chop clippings and blow them down to the base of the grass plant.

Lightweight reel mowers are a good non-polluting choice for small lawns. Look for mowers that allow you to adjust the mowing height without removing the wheels (inset).

Since their inception in the 1950s, rotary mowers have virtually replaced the reel mower for home lawns. They cut faster, they're less difficult to adjust or sharpen, and they do a better job of cutting tall, tough grass and weeds. Rotary mowers also usually offer a bigger selection of cutting heights than reel mowers, though most of them cannot cut lower than 1 inch.

All rotary mowers are power mowers. They may be either hand-pushed or self-propelled, walk-behind mowers or riding mowers. Riding mowers have much wider decks, up to 36 inches, compared to 18- to 22-inch widths for push or walk-behind mowers. With that width and their speed, riding mowers mow fast and are recommended for lawns of an acre or more. Their size may make maneuverability on small lots difficult, however, leaving lots of trim mowing for you to do by hand.

These days many rotary mowers are engineered as mulching mowers. Specially designed blades and decks cut clippings into fine particles, which decompose rapidly. There are conversion blades on the market to turn your conventional mower into a mulching mower. However, mulching mowers are more than a blade. Baffles in the deck keep the clippings aloft until finely chopped. The conversion blade may not do as good of a job.

Although they've been generally eclipsed by rotary mowers for the typical home lawn, reel mowers are still preferred for fine lawns. They conform better to land contours and their scissoring action produces a cleaner cut. They are especially useful for lawns of bentgrass and bermudagrass because they can be adjusted to cut quite low. However, reel mowers are impractical for mowing rough, uneven ground or tall grasses with high, wiry seed heads.

You may remember the heavy, bulky reel mowers of your youth, but if you haven't used one lately, you're in for a pleasant surprise. Made of durable lightweight materials, today's reel mowers weigh as little as 16 pounds, compared to 60 pounds for older reel mowers. Improved ball bearings, gears, and axles make them roll more smoothly. Height adjustment and blade adjustment have been simplified, and carbon steel blades hold an edge longer. The blades need sharpening only once every two years. You can take the mower to a shop for sharpening or do it yourself with a sharpening kit.

Reel mowers are available in several blade configurations, including four-, five-, or seven-blade designs. Seven-blade mowers are best for cutting low-growing, fine-textured grasses such as bermudagrass. Five-blade mowers are well suited for other grasses, while four-blade models are best for light use.

BUYING A MOWER

It pays to look around for the type of mower that fits your needs and to buy the highest-quality mower you can afford. A good mower should provide you with years of reliable service. Look for equipment that is large enough and powerful enough for the job. The money you save by buying a small, cheap machine may be insignificant compared to the extra time it takes to mow a lawn. For example, to cut a 1-acre lawn using a walk-behind with an 18-inch cutting width, it would take at least 2½ hours. A riding mower with a 36-inch width could do the job in about 30 minutes.

Before buying a lawn mower, carefully look it over. Consider its maneuverability, starting system, and features for adjusting handle and cutting height. Make sure the grass catcher is easy to put on and take off and that the safety shut-off handle fits your hand.

STRIPING THE LAWN

Anyone who's watched a baseball game on TV has wondered how the groundskeepers make those patterns in the grass. It's easy—if you have the right equipment.

The stripes are formed by using a reel mower and mowing one pass in one direction, the next in the opposite. With each pass, the mower blades and the rollers behind them push the blades in opposite directions.

Groundskeepers usually also follow up the mowing with a weighted roller, which they push down each stripe in the direction of the mowing to further knock over grass blades.

HOW TO KEEP AN EDGE

To cut cleanly, rotary mower blades should be sharpened about once a month under normal usage. Here's how to do it yourself.

First, remove the spark plug wire to prevent the mower from starting accidentally. Take off the blade by removing the nut that secures it to the mower deck. (You may have to wedge a piece of lumber between the blade and the deck to keep the blade from turning.)

Sharpen the edge of the blade using a file or a grindstone, following the angle of the edge. Take care to even out rough spots.

For a mower to run smoothly, the blade must be balanced. To check for balance, support the blade under its center.

THE WAY TO WATER

Lawns need up to one inch of water per week in order to thrive. If nature doesn't provide it, you'll have to step in and sprinkle. You must choose the sprinkler carefully though, considering flow rate, throw radius, and uniformity of coverage.

If your lawn shows footsteps after you walk across it, it's showing a need for water.

No matter where you live or what type of grass you grow, at some point you'll have to water the lawn. Exactly when and how often depends on several factors: your grass species, your soil type, your local climate, and the pattern of watering you have established in the past.

The water requirements for a given lawn can range from a minimum of ⅒ of an inch per day in a cool or shady location, to ½ inch per day in full sun, hot temperatures, high winds, and low humidity. But that does not mean you have to water every day.

The soil under the lawn has a lot to do with how often you need to water. Sandy soils do not hold water well, so a lawn grown on sand may have to be sprinkled two to three times a week if it doesn't rain. However, clay retains water well, and a lawn on a clay soil may require watering only once a week.

The lawn should be watered slowly, deeply, moistening soil to a depth of 6 to 12 inches, and as infrequently as possible. Running a sprinkler for a few minutes every evening is

WATER NEEDS OF GRASSES

Grass species vary considerably in the amount of moisture they require, and conversely, in how well they are able to grow in wet or dry soils. Here are the general water needs of the major turfgrass species.

DROUGHT-TOLERANT GRASSES
Cool Season
- Tall fescue
- Red fescue
- Some Kentucky bluegrasses
- Sheep fescue
- Hard fescue

Warm Season
- Buffalograss
- Blue gramagrass
- Common bermudagrass
- Hybrid bermudagrass
- Zoysiagrass

GRASSES THAT REQUIRE REGULAR WATERING
Cool Season
- Creeping bentgrass
- Colonial bentgrass

Warm Season
- St. Augustinegrass
- Carpetgrass

GRASSES TOLERANT OF WET SOILS
Cool Season
- Rough bluegrass
- Canada bluegrass

Warm Season
- St. Augustinegrass
- Carpetgrass

the worst way to water a lawn. Roots grow only where there is water, so if you consistently wet only the top few inches of soil, the roots do not venture any deeper. Eventually, the limited depth of the root system forces you into watering more often. That means trouble, because frequent watering keeps the surface wet, which is ideal for disease development. If roots go deep into the soil, they can draw on a larger underground water supply and the lawn can go much longer between waterings.

How do you know when the lawn needs water? It will tell you. The grass blades roll up lengthwise to conserve moisture. At the same time, they lose their bright green color, and the entire lawn may take on a grayish cast. Thirsty grass plants also lose their resiliency, so if you walk across a lawn in need of water, the grass will not spring back, and your footprints will remain visible.

WATER-SAVING TIPS

■ Water early in the morning. Watering at midday can waste water through evaporation.

■ Aerate your lawn before dry weather arrives to improve its drainage and moisture-holding capacity.

■ Avoid overfertilizing. Excessive nitrogen causes a growth spurt so the plant requires more water.

■ Increase your mowing height by about ½ inch. This extra height helps to shade the crowns of the plants during hot, dry weather.

■ Pull or spot-spray weeds to eliminate them and prevent them from competing with grass for moisture.

LIGHT WATERING PRODUCES SHALLOW ROOTS. HEAVY WATERING PRODUCES DEEP ROOTS.

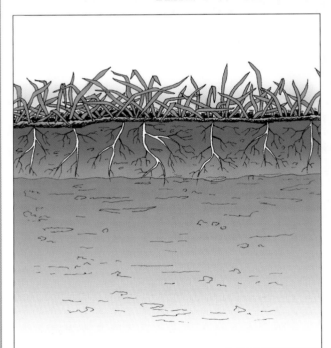

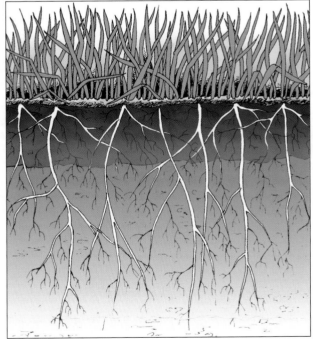

You may think you're doing your lawn a favor by sprinkling lightly every day or two, but you're not. Light watering wets only the top layer of soil. If it's done regularly, the grass roots "become accustomed" to finding water there, and grow shallowly. In times of drought, the plant then can't access deeper water.

Correct watering—applying at least one inch of water at one time—soaks the soil so that the water penetrates deeply. In this case, the roots don't "learn" to stay near the surface and penetrate deep into the soil where they can gather water even when the top of the soil dries out.

SHOPPING FOR SPRINKLERS

There are four basic types of portable sprinklers, each with its own means of delivering water to your lawn and with its own strengths and weaknesses. When shopping for a sprinkler, you should consider several factors, including the size of your lawn, the type of soil, and how often you water. Match the characteristics of the sprinkler to those conditions.

Choose a sprinkler that offers uniform coverage. If you have a large yard, you'll want a sprinkler with a long throw radius—the amount of ground the water spray covers—so that you don't have to move the sprinkler too often. In general, a sprinkler with a slow flow rate is best because it prevents wasteful water runoff.

When shopping for sprinklers, be aware that different brands of the same type of sprinkler vary considerably in their precision and performance, as well as durability and ease of use.

STATIONARY SPRINKLERS spray water in a fixed pattern through a small metal or plastic chamber pierced with holes. They are perhaps the least-efficient sprinklers because their uniformity is poor, and their throw radius is often short. Their flow rates may vary greatly. At the perimeter of the spray pattern, the grass may receive 8 inches an hour while closer to the sprinkler, it may get only 2 inches of water an hour. The area next to the sprinkler may stay dry. Stationary sprinklers are best used for spot watering or to supplement other types of sprinklers.

OSCILLATING SPRINKLERS throw water through an arched, perforated pipe that sweeps back and forth, delivering the water in a rectangular pattern. In general, their throw radius and uniformity are good. Older models had the fault of depositing most of the water near the sprinkler head. Newer versions have solved this problem by stalling momentarily when the arm is farthest from the upright

SPRINKLER GLOSSARY

FLOW RATE: The amount of water delivered by a sprinkler per hour. In general, the lower the flow rate the better.

THROW RADIUS: The amount of area covered by a sprinkler.

PATTERN: The shape of the area watered by the sprinkler. You should match the pattern to the shape of your lawn to avoid over- or underwatering areas.

UNIFORMITY: A measure of how consistently water falls at various locations within the throw pattern.

ON AGAIN, OFF AGAIN WATERING

If water puddles up and runs off your lawn, despite adjusting the water pressure, the flow rate of your sprinkler exceeds the ability of the soil to soak up water. Aside from buying a more efficient sprinkler, there is a technique you can use to solve this problem.

Rather than watering over one long period, cycle the watering. Try running your sprinkler for 15 minutes. Then leave it off for an hour to let the water soak in. Run the sprinkler for another 15-minute period followed by another hour off. Repeat this procedure until you have run the sprinkler for a total of one hour.

position, which allows more water to reach the outer boundaries. It's also easier to adjust the watering pattern on newer models, and some models also let you change the width of the watering area.

REVOLVING sprinklers shoot jets of water in a circular pattern from one or more rotating arms. Most models have a fair throw radius but relatively poor uniformity. The amount of water delivered decreases with the distance from the sprinkler, with most of the water falling between 4 and 8 feet out.

IMPULSE or impact sprinklers rotate through the combined action of an internal jet and an external hammer, delivering pulses of water in an adjustable circular pattern. The head can be set to send out a strong jet, a gentle mist, or anything in between. This type of sprinkler is a good choice for large areas. It is used on golf courses and in parks because of its uniform coverage.

TRAVELING SPRINKLERS use the same mechanism as revolving sprinklers: spinning arms that shoot out water. However, as the name implies, the entire sprinkler housing travels over the lawn, following a path laid out by the hose. Consequently, they offer thorough coverage, and their precipitation rate is generally good.

IN-GROUND SPRINKLER SYSTEMS offer convenience and efficiency. Spray heads pop up when the sprinkler is activated, often by an automatic timer. The heads are usually either a revolving or fixed type but provide much more uniform coverage. The system must be designed so that the spray heads are installed at correct intervals to provide full coverage of the lawn. Because of this and the labor involved, its best if professionals install them.

Fixed sprinklers spray water from a series of pinholes in the sprinkler head. The water pattern may range from square to rectangle to circular or semicircular. In fact, some fixed sprinklers have adjustable heads to provide a number of different patterns.

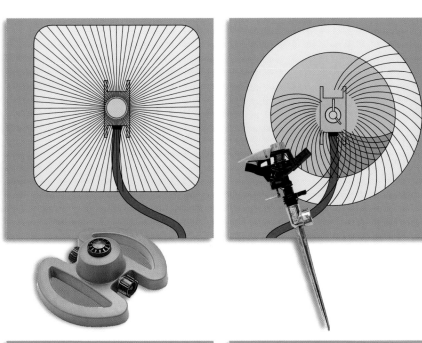

Impulse sprinklers shoot a stream of water from a jet nozzle, and the water is broken up into drops by a spring-loaded arm. These sprinklers usually throw water in a circular pattern, and most models may be adjusted to water only part of a circle.

Oscillating sprinklers shoot water from a slowly sweeping arm. Their normal pattern is rectangular, though most can be adjusted to throw water along a portion of the sweep. Because the spray shoots high into the air, wind easily deforms the water pattern.

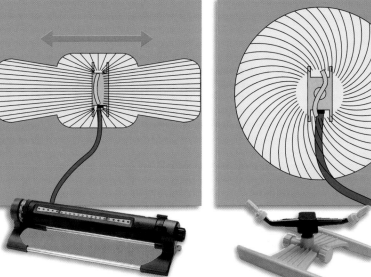

Revolving sprinklers shoot streams of water from a pair of spinning sprinkler nozzles. Because of this revolving motion, the pattern is always circular, and it is usually not adjustable. Also, more water falls on the outer edge of the circle than close to the sprinkler.

Traveling sprinklers operate like revolving sprinklers, spraying water from spinning arms, but with one difference: The entire unit moves across the lawn. Consequently, the water falls in a series of connecting circles, so the amount applied is more uniform.

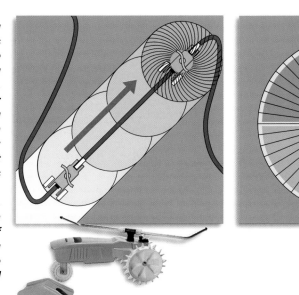

You can select a variety of sprinkler heads for underground or in-ground systems. Heads are stationary or revolving and can be set to water quarter- to full-circle areas or square or rectangular strips. Pop-up heads, such as this, are commonly used on small to medium lawns.

MORE LAWN CHORES

Compacted soil

Porous uncompacted soil

The tight pores of compacted soil prevent root growth.

Roots tend to grow in thatch, where they easily succumb to environmental stresses.

Power aerator

Foot aerator

Power thatcher

Cavex rake

Power trimmer

Aside from the big three—fertilizing, mowing, and watering—you may need to perform two other chores, especially if you maintain your lawn on a medium- or high-maintenance program. These are aerating and dethatching.

AERATING

Many lawns, particularly heavily used ones, have compacted soil, which restricts the movement of air and water to roots. The soil under lawns tends to compact readily because, unlike garden soil, it is virtually never worked or turned. For the lawn, aerating is the alternative to tilling.

Intensively maintained lawns should be aerated twice a year; those that receive moderate maintenance, once a year. Lawns with heavily compacted soil or severe thatch problems may also need twice-yearly aeration.

Aerating is really a simple process. It consists of perforating the soil (and any thatch above it) with small holes, which allow water, air, and fertilizer to get to roots. Aerating enables the roots to grow deeply and produce a more vigorous lawn.

Several types of tools are available for aerating lawns.

If your lawn is small, there's a foot-press aerator that you push into the soil like a spade. For larger lawns, you can buy or rent an engine-powered aerator. They resemble lawn mowers, and you steer them across the lawn, aerating as you go.

Aerating tools remove thin cigar-shaped plugs of soil and deposit them on the surface of the lawn. Leave them there to dry for a day or so, then break them up with energetic raking to create a thin, beneficial topdressing. Make sure that the soil is moist, but not too wet, during aeration so the aerator can penetrate easily.

DETHATCHING

Thatch develops when dead organic matter—grass stems, dead roots, and debris but not clippings—builds up faster than it decomposes. It accumulates on top of the soil at the base of the blades.

The causes of thatch are numerous: poorly aerated soil, excess nitrogen, or too-high or too-infrequent mowing. It also results from growing a vigorous cultivar and using pesticides that kill earthworms and microflora that break down organic matter.

On a well-maintained lawn, thatch is rarely a problem. A thin layer (½ inch or less) is normal and does no harm. In fact, it protects the crown

No thatch

Thatch

Power edger   **Hand edger**

and reduces soil compaction. A layer thicker than ½ inch prevents water from reaching the roots. If your lawn feels spongy when you walk on it, it has excessive thatch.

Because severe dethatching can weaken turf, it's better to deal with the problem before such action is necessary. The best time to dethatch is just before grass begins its most vigorous growth.

There are several ways to do it. For lawns with moderate thatch, simply aerating the lawn will do the trick. For small lawns, use a thatching or cavex rake to take up the thatch. The long knifelike blades of these specialized

rakes cut through the sod and pull up thatch. For large lawns with serious thatch problems, the most effective solution is a vertical mower. Resembling a heavy-duty power mower, this machine has a series of revolving vertical knives that cut and pull through the thatch, bringing it to the surface. Rake up the material afterwards.

Edging and trimming aren't necessary tasks, but they add a finished touch to the lawn. Keep edges sharp and clean with either a hand- or power-edging tool. Use a string trimmer, either electric- or gasoline-powered, to trim corners and mower-inaccessible spots.

LAWN CARE CALENDAR

Most of us tend our lawns according to a schedule that suits us. Usually that means doing yard work once a week whether the lawn needs it or not. We mow, fertilize, and water when we have a chance. However, our schedules may not always suit the needs of the lawn.

All lawns differ somewhat in the timing for certain tasks, but the following is a general guideline for chores you should be thinking about over the course of the season. The maintenance regime you follow—low, moderate or high—will determine whether you actually do each task.

COOL-SEASON TURFGRASSES

Spring:
■ Examine lawns for signs of disease and insects (see pages 76 and 84).
■ Mow at the minimum height to enhance turf density. (See page 41 for proper mowing heights.) Mow whenever the grass height increases by one-third, perhaps as often as twice a week.
■ If thatch layer is deeper than ½ inch, dethatch.
■ Aerate if necessary.
■ Establish new lawns or patch bare spots in existing lawns.
■ Fertilize using a material with 75 percent of the nitrogen in a slow-release form.

■ Treat with a pre-emergence herbicide for grassy weeds if needed.
Summer:
■ Examine lawns for signs of disease and insects.
■ Raise mower deck and cut at maximum height to enhance stress tolerance.
■ Deep water as necessary.
■ If weeds are troublesome, use a grass catcher to collect clippings and weed seeds. Apply post-emergence broadleaf herbicide if desired.
■ Edge and trim as desired.
Early autumn:
■ Lower mower deck to cut at minimum height.
■ Fertilize.
■ Sow new cool-season lawn, or reseed bare patches in the lawn. This is the best time for this task.
Late autumn:
■ Continue mowing at maximum height, taking off no more than a third at a time so grass is well insulated in winter.
■ For medium- or high-maintenance lawns, apply a third dose of fertilizer.

WARM-SEASON TURFGRASSES

Early spring:
■ Apply pre-emergence herbicide for grassy weeds as needed.

Spring:
■ Examine lawns for signs of disease and insects.
■ Aerate and dethatch after lawn breaks dormancy.
■ Make first mowing when the lawn breaks dormancy at the lowest recommended height to remove brown blade tips.
■ Fertilize when the lawn breaks dormancy.
Summer:
■ Examine lawns for signs of disease and insects.
■ Raise the height of the mower deck to the maximum height and mow often enough to remove only a third of the blade at a time.
■ Fertilize.
■ Establish new lawns or patch bare spots in existing lawns.
■ If weeds are troublesome, use a grass catcher to collect clippings and weed seeds. Apply post-emergence herbicide for broadleaf weeds if desired.
■ Water deeply as necessary.
■ Edge and trim as necessary.
Autumn:
■ Examine lawns for signs of disease and insects.
■ Continue mowing as necessary but delay mowing as growth slows so that grass goes into winter well insulated.
■ Overseed with cool-season grasses for winter color.

BUILDING A BETTER LAWN

Lawn that's less than 50 percent good grass (left): start over. Thin, spotty turf that's in decent health (center): rejuvenate. Thick, healthy grass with a few spots or weeds (right): fine-tune maintenance.

If you're just not happy with your lawn, the grass seems to struggle no matter what you do, you have to face the question: Can this lawn be saved, or is it time to start all over from scratch?

The answer to that question lies with a thorough examination of your lawn. Start by focusing on individual grass plants. Are they a fine-bladed turfgrass with good green color and a generally healthy appearance? If so, the lawn is probably worth saving. However, if the grass is a coarse-bladed pasture grass, naturally pale green or frequently marred by

disease and insects, there's little you can do to make it look better. It might be best to start over.

Next, examine the overall lawn. Is the turf unattractive because it's comprised of a mish-mash of unmatched grasses? If so, start over.

How about diseases? If you're constantly dealing with brown patches, circles of dying grass, and other symptoms of disease, you have an underlying problem. You can either start over or overseed with a resistant grass, which will eventually become the dominant grass in the stand.

Is the sod thick or thin? You shouldn't be able to see bare ground between grass plants. And if the lawn is thin, chances are weeds have moved in to fill the available space.

If you can see bare soil but the plants seem healthy and are aesthetically pleasing, you may not need to start from scratch. Overseeding might be enough to thicken the lawn.

But if more than 50 percent of the lawn is bare, weed infested, diseased, or has other problems, it's probably worthwhile to dig it up and replace it. Less than 50 percent, you can get by with merely repairing the problem area.

Before repairing or replacing the lawn, you must correct the underlying cause. Otherwise, the new grass will end up with the same problems. So, the next step is to look for causes. One of the first places to check is the soil, which is the source of many lawn problems. Test its fertility, as explained on page 58, and look for thatch and compacted layers. If the soil needs drastic reworking, you'll have to remove the lawn to get to it, but first, you might want to try aerating and fertilizing.

CAN THIS LAWN BE SAVED?

If your lawn seems to be struggling no matter what you do, you may be tempted to throw up your hands, remove the lawn, and start all over. However, even if your lawn is troublesome, it may not require such a drastic step. Before you bust the sod, answer these questions to determine whether your lawn indeed must be replaced or if you can repair it instead.

REPLACE THE LAWN?

If you answer yes to any of these questions, you should probably consider replacing the grass in your lawn with a species and variety suited to the conditions of your landscape.

■ Are you trying to grow the wrong grass for your climate and your lawn, for example, bermudagrass on the northern edge of the transition zone?
■ Does your lawn regularly turn brown during summer?
■ Is your lawn the last one in the neighborhood to green up in spring or the first to turn brown in fall?
■ Is the grass outpaced by weeds in spring?
■ Do warm-season weeds such as crabgrass present a constant battle despite control measures?
■ Is most of the turf coarse bladed and pale colored?
■ Is your lawn a series of patches of three or more different colored and textured grasses?
■ Do insects (other than grubs) leave large dying or dead patches in your lawn?
■ Does water puddle up throughout the lawn after a rain, causing the grass to turn yellow and lose vigor? Or does the grass wilt and take on a grayish cast if it's not watered regularly?

Use the glossary information on pages 12 to 25 to choose an appropriate turfgrass species for your conditions. If your lawn particularly has problems with insects, replant with an improved, insect-resistant variety.

Severe and consistent weed infestations and diseases are signs of underlying problems, such as poor soil. Use the method described on page 28 to determine the percentage of weeds in your lawn. If your lawn consists of more than 50 percent weeds, it's best to replace it. If diseases occur throughout the lawn at least once annually, it's time to install a new lawn of disease-resistant grasses.

Water puddling on the soil surface and wilting turf indicate the soil needs improvement. To do so, you'll have to remove the turf for best results.

After selecting an appropriate grass species and correcting underlying problems, follow the instructions on pages 58 to 63 for installing a new lawn.

REPAIR YOUR LAWN?

Less serious lawn problems require less drastic action. You should make the choice to repair your existing lawn if:
■ Most of the grass is fine-bladed and deep green.
■ The grass may be slightly thin but is generally healthy.
■ The lawn is less than 25 percent weeds.
■ Diseases occur only occasionally if at all.
■ Grass turns brown only during the most severe droughts.

Repairing your lawn may consist of adjusting your fertilizing and watering regime, overseeding with new varieties, aerating, and topdressing.

REPAIRING THE LAWN BY OVERSEEDING

If you'd like your lawn to be thicker, greener, more fine-bladed, as well as more vigorous and stress-tolerant, there's one relatively simple solution: Reseed it with a new, improved variety. At first thought, that seems like an intimidating prospect, but it doesn't necessarily mean that you have to dig up and replace your old lawn with a new one.

There's an easier way: overseed the existing lawn with new seed. You'll take advantage of the vigor and vitality of these new grasses, and if you choose a variety that's well adapted to your conditions, it will become established in your existing lawn and, in time, crowd out the older, weaker varieties.

Before overseeding, analyze the condition of your current lawn. If it is a wreck, with less than 50 percent good grass, your best choice is to remove the existing turf and start over. However, if strong, vigorous grass comprises more than 60 percent of the lawn, then overseeding might be a viable option. Next, try to determine the causes of the deterioration of your existing turf. Is it shade?

If your lawn is thin, but not too weedy, and the existing grass is attractive and healthy, you may not need to start a new lawn from scratch.

Rather than replacing the entire lawn, you can repair it by overseeding. The lawn above has new life (right) since it was reseeded with a new variety of grass right over the old, existing lawn.

Drought? Insects or disease? Only after you've determined the cause can you choose the appropriate new grass for overseeding. For example, select a shade-tolerant fescue for shady lawns, or an insect-resistant perennial ryegrass if insect infestations have ruined your cool-season lawn. In the case of recurring diseases, you may have to call in a professional to make a diagnosis, then choose a new variety resistant to that disease.

Of course, you can't just spread the seed and expect it to find fertile ground on its own. You have to do a little prep work first, and then be prepared to do some follow-up care.

First, choose the best time for germination. That's fall for cool-season turfgrasses and spring for warm-season grasses. (For overseeding Southern lawns for winter color, see box on this page.) Then follow the steps for overseeding below. Once established, continue with your normal feeding, watering, and mowing regime, and in time, the new grasses will take over the lawn.

STEP-BY-STEP OVERSEEDING

The success of overseeding depends on making sure the seed contacts the soil. To ensure this happens, prepare the old lawn by mowing it as closely as possible (A). Rake up the clippings, then mow and rake again. This helps expose the soil.

Next, scratch the soil vigorously with a metal garden rake to rough it up and create a good seed bed (B).

Because you're not sowing into bare ground, you'll need to sow seed at two to three times the amount recommended on the package. (C) If you have a weighted roller handy, firm the seed into the soil with it. Then cover the seed with a thin, 1/4–1/2 inch, layer of topsoil or finely ground compost. Water daily until the seed germinates.

Mowing helps the new lawn fill in. When the new seedlings emerge, allow them to grow to the maximum cutting height. Then mow (D). Don't let seedlings grow too tall so that you end up taking off more than one-third of their height.

OVERSEEDING FOR WINTER COLOR

In the South, warm-season grasses go dormant early in winter, leaving you with a brown lawn the rest of the season. Because cool-season grasses thrive in the temperatures of a Southern winter, you can sow them over warm-season grasses for temporary color.

Choose a vigorous grass that germinates quickly in fall and dies back as the warm-season grass greens up in spring. If the cool-season grass grows too late in spring, it could compete with the warm-season species. Perennial ryegrass and red fescue are two popular species fitting this criteria.

Sow seed when temperatures begin to drop, usually in October or November. If you start too early, still active warm-season grasses crowd out the cool-season grass. Start too late and cold weather may inhibit germination.

The next spring, encourage the regrowth of the warm-season grass by closely mowing the cool-season cover. The latter will die out as the temperature rises.

PATCHING THE LAWN

To repair a spot, first square off the area by slicing through the turf with a spade, cutting 6 inches into good grass. Dispose of the sod.

Next, prepare soil as thoroughly as when starting a lawn. Remove debris, add organic matter and fertilizer, then smooth and level the soil with a rake.

Perhaps most of your lawn is in good condition with only a few troublesome spots, such as a weedy patch or a bare area. In this case, you don't need to replace or overseed the entire lawn. You can patch the damaged area.

MAKE CORRECTIONS FIRST

Before doing anything, figure out what has led to the damage, especially if it's a chronic spot and not one resulting from a one-time accident, such as spilling hot charcoals on the grass. Unless you correct the underlying cause, you'll be faced with the same symptoms over and over again.

There are a number of possible reasons for bad patches in the lawn. Weedy turf could be due to soil compaction. Thin turf could result from shade or poor drainage. Heavy traffic or frequent use creates bare areas. A patch of

yellow could result from fertilizer, herbicide, gasoline spills, or from the family dog.

To reduce compaction, aerate the soil as described on page 48. Trim trees and shrubs to let in more light, or if that's impractical, sow a shade-tolerant species. (In large areas, you'll find it easier to overseed than to make spot repairs.) For fertilizer and other spills, flush the soil well with water (see page 90).

Finally, patch the area by sowing seed. Use a grass species or variety that matches the existing lawn. That is, make sure that it is similar in texture, color, and cultural requirements to the existing grass.

PREPARE THE SOIL

Once you've corrected the problem, it's time to begin the repair process. The first step is to prepare a good seed bed for the grass (even if you will be patching the area with sod, sprigs, or plugs).

Completely remove whatever grass or weed cover exists in the problem area. Then, square off the area to make patching more convenient. For best results, enlarge the area about 6 inches beyond the problem itself.

Next, prepare the soil as thoroughly as you would if you were replanting a new lawn. Turn it to a depth of 6 inches, removing any weed roots or rhizomes or any other debris, such as rocks or tree roots, in the soil.

If the soil is sand or heavy clay, add several inches of compost or other organic matter, and mix it into the soil well. Finally, rake the surface to level it, then water well.

REPLANT

BY SEED: Now it's time to replant. If you're repairing the patch with seed, sow it at the recommended rate, then rake to cover with a thin layer of soil. (In hot, dry weather, also

BY SPRIGS AND PLUGS: Some grasses are available as sprigs or plugs, which are ideal for repairing or patching the lawn. Sprigs, also called stolons or runners, are small pieces of grass plants, complete with crowns and roots. Plugs are small, round patches of sod about 2 to 4 inches around.

Generally, you plant sprigs 4 to 12 inches apart, depending on species, and plugs 6 to 12 inches apart. However, for patching, you can space them closer together, which will allow them to fill in bare spots faster.

Prepare the soil as for sowing seed or sodding, but take extra care after planting sprigs and plugs. The soil must be kept evenly moist for about one month to allow their roots to become established. You must also be diligent about keeping the bare area between the sprigs or plugs weed free until the new grass has completely covered the bare ground.

The fastest way to patch a lawn is with sod. Cut the sod to match the prepared area, then lay it so that its edges touch those of the existing grass. Firm the sod into the soil.

To patch with plugs—small patches of sod— plant them 2 to 4 inches apart, making sure the roots are completely covered with soil.

To patch with sprigs—small pieces of grass— scatter them over the area 4 to 10 inches apart. Press the sprigs into the soil, then mulch.

cover the seed with a light layer of weed-free mulch.) Keep the soil moist until the seed germinates. After the seed germinates, leave the grass unmown until it reaches its maximum recommended height.

BY SOD: Cut pieces of sod to match the area that you cut around the damage, and lay it as described on page 62.

NEW LAWNS: DESIGN

Often, existing lawns have problem spots that will never support good turf growth. It's better to redesign the lawn to turn the problems into successes. For example, you can take a worn-out, difficult to mow yard like the one in the illustration on page 57 and turn it into a beautiful landscape like the one above.

The lawn and plantings you install today will be with you for years to come. So before doing any work, take time to make a plan for the lawn. Think about the practical things, for example, how you intend to use your yard and how easy the lawn should be to maintain. Consider where traffic patterns will be, say from the house to the mail box or to the water faucet, and where the children will play or where you want to practice your golf swing. Planning now can reduce the number of problems you have with the lawn later on.

There are several ways to reduce future maintenance chores while creating a pleasing design. For example, if trees are in lawn areas, group them together in large beds with shrubs and ground covers. At the very least, you should create a wide, mulched area around each tree to avoid nicking bark with the mower as well as to make mowing easier. These mulched areas also help the tree become established faster because they eliminate competition between tree and grass roots.

In areas that will be heavily trafficked, use paving or other hardscaping from the start. Then there'll be no need to repair or replace the "cow paths" that develop. Use a wear-tolerant turfgrass in play areas or consider mulching the area instead of planting grass.

To simplify mowing, avoid creating awkward corners among the plantings. Also, make sure every patch of lawn is accessible with the mower. Trying to get the mower up stairs or through a narrow passage will make mowing a less desirable chore.

Be sure to consider the terrain and microclimates of your yard. For example, grass seed tends to wash away on slopes, and slopes are dangerous to mow and difficult to adequately water. Planting ground covers rather than turfgrass may be the most appropriate solution for a slope.

Think about future irrigation needs when planning your lawn, too. If watering with a hose-end sprinkler, avoid creating nooks and crannies that will require extra fussing with the sprinkler to avoid dry spots in the lawn.

NEW LAWN PLAN

The failure of many lawns is often due to their design and placement. Perhaps the lawn is too large for you to manage properly. Or maybe parts of your yard are deeply shaded or extremely wet or dry—areas where few turf varieties are adapted to grow. It could also be that your activities—such as the kids playing football or simply walking between the house and the garage—put too much wear and tear on the lawn.

If your lawn is doing poorly, take a look at how it fits the landscape. Although it's true that in most circumstances, nothing can beat a lawn, there are some conditions in which other materials might be better. For example, it may be better to replace the worn paths in the grass with stone, gravel, or pavement. Where the grass has thinned from deep shade, you'd be better off installing a shade-tolerant border of shrubs, perennials, or ground cover. Where trees grow in the middle of the lawn, build a bed around them with shrubs, ground covers, and mulch.

What it boils down to is this: Rather than forcing the lawn to grow where it can't do well, sacrifice some of it for the good of the whole.

SHRINKING THE LAWN

Redesigning the landscape to reduce maintenance, can lead to another problem: How do you get rid of the existing grass? In fact, removing a lawn, or part of it, can be as much hard work—if not more—as installing one in the first place. Luckily, you have several options.

■ Non-selective herbicides, such as products containing glyphosate, kill the grass and all other vegetation. Herbicides work quickly and require virtually no physical labor. When applying the herbicide, take care to keep the spray off nearby plants. Cover them with a tarp or use some other physical barrier. Also avoid spraying on windy days when fine sprays can drift long distances. Don't spray in very hot weather, either. Some herbicides can volatilize and affect nearby plants.

■ You can remove sod manually, using a spade in small areas or with a rented sod stripper.

■ Solarizing is a good, low-tech way to remove turf. When weather is hot and sunny, cover the area tightly with clear plastic and leave it on for a few weeks. High temperatures under the plastic will kill the lawn, other plants, and weed seeds.

■ One last option: Spread several pages of newspaper on the soil, then cover them with bark or other mulch to shade out turf and weeds.

FOR NEW LAWNS, START WITH THE SOIL

Starting a new lawn from scratch offers a great opportunity to improve the soil beneath it. So don't scrimp on this chance to get the soil right before putting in your new grass.

TEST SOIL FIRST

The first step in preparing to install a lawn is to have your soil tested. A soil test eliminates any guesswork about what amendments are required and will give you exact information about pH and nutrient deficiencies and the presence of organic matter and harmful salts.

Many universities and county extension offices test soils for residents. Contact your local extension office for details. Private labs also do the tests; if none are listed in the phone book, call your extension office for recommendations.

Some labs tell you only the levels of major and micronutrients in the soil. Others supply instructions on how to interpret test results and what steps to take to improve the soil.

To get reliable test results, gather samples from 10 to 20 spots around the yard. Take them with a core sampler. Push this tube-like device into damp ground to pull out a plug of soil about ¾ inches in diameter and 4 to 12 inches long. If you do not have a core sampler, use a clean trowel or shovel to take the samples.

Before sampling, scrape off the top 4 to 6 inches of soil from the spot. Insert the sampler, then place the core in a clean bucket. Mix the samples together, then measure about a pint of this mixture and put it in the container provided by the soil lab. Label the container and mail it to the lab. If you have problem areas, sample and send them separately.

While waiting for the results, you can begin preparing the soil. First, remove all debris such as wood, stones, and large roots. Next, use a garden rake to establish a rough grade by filling in low spots and leveling hills. Measure the size of the lawn, according to the instructions in the box on the next page.

Once the results arrive, you're ready to add soil amendments. Spread the amount of fertilizer recommended in your soil test results, and work it into the soil to a depth

Consult your soil test and apply the correct amount of fertilizer, then add organic matter. It's best to work amendments 4 to 6 inches into the soil. Do this by hand with a shovel in small areas. In large areas, a tiller works best.

of 4 to 8 inches. The easiest way to do this is with a rotary tiller. While you're at it, work in organic matter (see page 59), especially if the soil is sand or clay. However, do not add materials high in carbon—sawdust, wood chips, or straw. They will rob the nitrogen from the soil.

After tilling, grade the soil, then firm it with a roller. Water the soil, then let it settle for about a week. Finally, smooth over any rough spots that develop and do the final grade on the soil, making sure it is level throughout the entire area.

Prepare the bare soil by removing all debris such as stones, twigs and roots. Use a rake to level the soil and establish a rough grade.

After mixing in the amendments, do the final grade on the soil. When you're done, the soil should be level with no high or low spots. You'll find using a long aluminum landscape rake will make the task go faster.

ADDING ORGANIC MATTER

Many lawns are sadly deficient in organic matter. Too often, lawns are sown in subsoil after the topsoil has been removed. And even when lawns have been started in good soil, the organic matter level decreases over the years. A lack of organic matter contributes to compaction, poor drainage and water-holding capacity, and by extension, excessive dryness or wetness. On the other hand, soils with a good organic matter content increase fertilizer availability, and plants grown in them are often more resistant to diseases.

Topdressing with compost is an easy way to regularly replenish the organic matter in your soil. But for seriously deficient soils, you may want to work in more than the shallow layer that topdressing adds. Use the following chart to determine how much organic matter to put on. (One cubic yard covers 162 square feet to a depth of 2 inches.)

Area in square feet	Cubic yards of organic matter to mix into the top 6 inches of soil to achieve 10, 15, 20, 25 or 30 percent organic matter				
	10%	15%	20%	25%	30%
300	0.6	0.8	1.1	1.4	1.7
500	0.9	1.4	1.9	2.3	2.8
1,000	1.9	2.8	3.7	4.6	5.6
3,000	5.6	8.3	11.1	13.9	16.7
5,000	9.3	13.9	18.5	23.1	27.8
10,000	18.5	27.8	37.0	46.3	55.6
20,000	37.0	55.6	74.1	92.6	111.1
40,000	74.1	111.1	148.1	185.2	222.2

MEASURING YOUR LAWN

You'll need to know the size of your lawn for many cultural practices, including watering and fertilizing. If the lawn is a square or rectangle, the measurement is rather straightforward. Use standard geometric calculations. For other shapes, you'll have to use a bit more geometry.

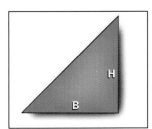

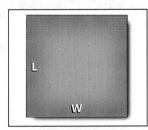

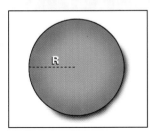

SQUARE OR RECTANGLE
Area = L times W
L = Length
W = Width

Example:
A = 90 feet × 60 feet
A = 5,400 square feet

CIRCLE
Area = πr^2
π = 3.14
r^2 = radius squared

Example:
A = 3.14 × 20 feet × 20 feet
A = 1,256 square feet

TRIANGLE
Area = 0.5 times B times H
B = Base
H = Height

Example:
A = 0.5 × 60 feet × 120 feet
A = 3,600 square feet

IRREGULAR SHAPES (accuracy within 5%)
Mark the length (L) of the area. Every 10 feet along the length line, measure the width (W) at right angles to the length line. Add up these measurements and multiply the result by 10.
Example:
A = W1 + W2 + W3, etc. × 10
A = 132 × 10
A = 1,320 square feet

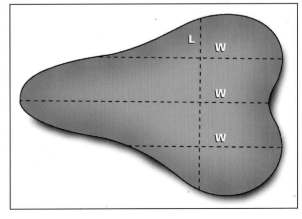

STARTING NEW LAWNS FROM SEED

Just before you sow the lawn, you should use a metal garden rake to comb out any remaining rocks and make the surface as even as possible. Then roll it lightly with a lawn roller about half full of water.

Finally, it's time to sow the seed. Calculate the amount you will need to cover the space you've prepared. (If you are planting an acre or more of lawn, you can seed in sections.) For large areas, use either a broadcast or drop spreader. In small areas, you can easily sow the seed by hand. Regardless of the seeding method, take care to get uniform coverage.

Before you begin, divide the recommended amount of seed into two equal lots. Sow the first lot across the lawn in rows, then sow the second lot in rows at right angles to the first until you have crisscrossed the whole lawn. If you are using a fertilizer spreader, calibrate it to deliver the total amount of seed at half the recommended rate in each direction.

After seeding, ensure good contact between seed and soil by lightly raking the entire area. Then go over it with a water-filled roller. Don't rake too roughly. Doing so could redistribute the seed, ruin the final grade and bury the seed too deeply.

Mulch after seeding to keep the soil moist and hasten germination. You may use any number of materials: finely shredded compost or dried manure, topsoil, straw, or even a thin

Using the instructions on the seed package, determine the amount of seed required for the square footage of your lawn. To ensure uniformity, apply one-half the amount required in the first pass; the rest in a second pass.

Push the spreader across the lawn, overlapping passes 2 to 4 inches. Make one pass, then go over the lawn again at right angles.

After sowing the seed, water it in well so that soil is wet to a depth of 4 to 6 inches. Then cover the area with a light layer of clean, weed-free mulch to keep the soil moist.

SEEDING RATES

Grass species	Pounds of seed per 1,000 square feet	Days to germinate
Bahiagrass	8–10	21–28
Creeping bentgrass	½–1	4 – 12
Common bermudagrass	1–2	10–30
Blue gramagrass	1–3	15–30
Kentucky bluegrass	1–2	14–30
Buffalograss	2	14–30
Centipedegrass	1–2	14–30
Fine fescues	2–5	7–14
Tall fescue	6–10	7–12
Perennial ryegrass	5–10	5–10

layer of sawdust. Apply the mulch no more than ¼ inch thick and as evenly as possible. Then begin watering.

For seed to germinate consistently, the top layer of soil must stay constantly moist. Mulch will help but won't get you off the hook. You must thoroughly soak the soil to a 6-inch depth after sowing, then lightly water with a sprinkler as often as three to four times daily until the grass is established. Even a short dry period can kill the germinating seed. Use a fine spray or nozzle with a mist setting to avoid washing away soil and seed.

Allow the young grass to reach its maximum recommended height (see the chart on page 41) before mowing.

MIXES AND BLENDS

Most cool-season grasses are sold as mixtures (a combination of two or more species) or blends (a combination of two or more varieties of the same species). Here are some typical mixtures for various conditions.

General purpose lawn in full sun: 50% Kentucky bluegrass and 50% red fescue, or 75% Kentucky bluegrass and 25% perennial ryegrass.

Shade: 60% fine fescue and 40% Kentucky bluegrass; or 40% Kentucky bluegrass, 40% red fescue, and 20% perennial ryegrass.

Cool, moist climates: 75% fine fescue and 25% 'Exeter' colonial bentgrass.

Wear-tolerant turf in sun or light shade: 30% Kentucky bluegrass, 20% perennial ryegrass, and 50% fine fescue.

Turf for heavily used areas: 10% Kentucky bluegrass and 90% turf-type tall fescue.

Moist, shady locations: 30% rough bluegrass, 30% Kentucky bluegrass, 20% fine fescue, and 20% perennial ryegrass.

For a fast-establishing lawn: 50% Kentucky bluegrass and 50% perennial ryegrass.

For year-round color in warm-season areas: 25% zoysiagrass and 75% turf-type tall fescue.

READING A SEED LABEL

A certain amount of information is required to appear on all grass seed labels, but you may have a hard time interpreting it. Here's a look at a sample seed label and what the words mean:

TYPE OF GRASS
Look for high-quality turfgrasses. Here, "improved tall fescue blend" tells you that the seed is composed of newer turf-type tall fescues and that there is more than one variety of tall fescue in the bag.

VARIETY
Named varieties are considered superior to common types and in most cases are a sign of a good mixture or blend.

GERMINATION PERCENTAGE
This represents the percentage of seed that germinates under ideal conditions. The percentage varies from species to species, and can deteriorate over time. Never buy seed with less than 70% germination.

PURE SEED PERCENTAGES
Percentages indicate the proportion of the grass by weight, not by seed count.

Inert Matter: Inert matter includes chaff, dirt, and miscellaneous material that manages to escape cleaning. It should not exceed 4 percent.

OTHER CROP SEED
This is seed of any commercially grown grass crop, such as timothy or orchardgrass. There should be no other crop seed in a good lawn mix.

WEED SEED
It is virtually impossible to keep all weed seeds out of a seed crop, but look for less than 1 percent.

```
LOT  NUMBER    75ENV07G
ENVIRO   TALL FESCUE   BLEND
PURE SEED   VARIETY     KIND        GERMINATION   ORIGIN
59%            DUSTER    TALL FESCUE      90%        OREGON
25%            VIRTUE    TALL FESCUE      90%        OREGON
14% FINELAWN PETITE  TALL FESCUE      90%        OREGON
1.00%   INERT MATTER
0.75%   OTHER CROP SEED      TEST DATE  4-98
0.25%   WEED SEED   NET WEIGHT   5  POUND
        NOXIOUS WEED SEED
NONE FOUND PER POUND

OTHER CROP SEED INCLUDES 0.50% RYEGRASS
```

ORIGIN
When seed quantities account for more than 5 percent of the mixture, the label must show the state or country where the seed crop was grown. This has no bearing on how well the grass will do in your yard.

TEST DATE
This is the guarantee that all the information listed on the label is correct. Buy seed that shows a date from the current year.

NOXIOUS WEEDS
Some especially troublesome weeds, such as field bindweed and others, are declared noxious by most states. It is illegal to sell seed that contains these weeds. If present, they must be individually named and the number of seeds per ounce indicated. A good mixture will contain no noxious weeds.

SODDING, SPRIGGING, AND PLUGGING NEW LAWNS

Sodding is the fastest way to make a new lawn. Measure your lawn and prepare the soil before ordering. When the sod arrives, make sure it is green throughout with no brown or dry patches. Each strip should also have a layer of soil and healthy white roots.

Seeding isn't the only way to start a lawn. The other options are sodding, sprigging, and plugging. You can sod many varieties of both cool- and warm-season turfgrasses, but several warm-season grasses are available only as sprigs or plugs.

SODDING

Sod offers a number of advantages over seed. You can sod a lawn at almost any time of the growing season (you don't have to wait for the best season, as you do when sowing seed) and you can sod where seed may be hard to establish, such as in areas with heavy foot traffic or on slopes. The main advantage to sodding the lawn is speed. A sod lawn can be useable in as little as three weeks.

Sodding doesn't mean you can skip any steps, however. You still have to prepare the soil just as carefully as you would when sowing seed.

PREPARATION: Order sod about a week before the planting date. This allows the grower to schedule cutting or the local nursery time to order from his supplier. It's

As you lay the sod, make sure that the pieces butt up tightly against one another, and that all of the roots are in firm contact with the soil.

If there are small, odd-shaped, hard-to-fill patches, cut the sod with a sharp knife to fit those spots.

not difficult to estimate the amount of sod you need: Simply determine your lawn's square footage, then have the nursery or grower calculate the number of rolls you need. Buy that amount plus 5 to 10 percent more to ensure you have enough.

If soil is dry, wet it thoroughly a few days before the sod is delivered, but allow the soil surface to dry before laying sod. Plan to lay the sod on the day it arrives; have the pallets stacked near the planting area, if possible. If you can't plant the same day, put the sod in a cool, shaded area and keep the outer rolls moist. Lay the sod as soon as possible.

LAYING: The easiest way to begin laying sod is to start near a straight edge, such as a sidewalk or driveway. If you have an irregularly shaped lawn, create a straight line by drawing one on it with spray paint or lime or by stringing a line across it.

Handle the sod strips carefully to avoid tearing or stretching them. When rolling them out, stand or kneel on a piece of plywood to distribute your weight evenly. Unroll the first roll. Butt the end of the second one tightly against the first and unroll it carefully. Repeat this process until you have laid one complete strip across your lawn.

With each successive strip, tightly fit both the ends and the edges against each other. Stagger the ends of the sod pieces, much as a bricklayer staggers bricks. After laying all the sod, roll a water-filled roller across it to ensure good contact between sod and soil.

After rolling the sod, water thoroughly. From then on, watch your new lawn closely. The edges of the sod strips will be the first to dry out, and may need daily watering. Make sure the underlying soil stays moist for at least the first two weeks.

SPRIGGING AND PLUGGING

A number of warm-season grasses, such as hybrid bermudagrass, do not set viable seed and can only be grown vegetatively, such as by sprigs and plugs. Sprigs (also called stolons or runners) are pieces of torn-up sod of creeping grasses. Plugs are small squares or circles of sod that are also planted at intervals. You plant each type several inches apart and eventually they grow together.

Sprig planting is best done from late spring to midsummer, and there are several ways to plant them. You can dig 2- to 3-inch-deep furrows, 4 to 12 inches apart, place the sprigs in the furrows, and firm the soil around each stem. You can also lay the sprigs out on the soil at desired intervals and lightly press them in with a notched stick. The fastest planting method is broadcast sprigging. Strew them over the soil by hand, then cover them with soil and roll lightly with a water-filled roller.

Plant sprigs in late spring or midsummer. After preparing the soil, scatter the sprigs 6 to 12 inches apart, 2 to 3 inches deep. Or plant them in individual holes or in 2-inch-deep furrows.

Plugs should be planted in early spring. Before they arrive, use a steel plugger (or a trowel or small spade) to dig holes of the proper size in the soil, spacing them 6 to 12 inches apart, depending on the size of the plugs and type of grass. To help the lawn take hold evenly, offset the rows of plugs in a checkerboard pattern.

When the plugs arrive, lightly moisten the soil and place the plugs in the holes. Firm the soil around them so that their crowns are level with the ground. After planting, roll them as with sod and sprigs.

Water sprigs and plugs daily for the first two weeks after planting so that they do not dry out. They may take up to two years to fill in completely, so it is vitally important to keep the soil between them free of weeds until they have filled in the lawn.

Sprigs are pieces of grass stems.

Plugs are little pieces of sod.

To start a new lawn using plugs, prepare the soil thoroughly, then use a sod plugging tool or a small spade to dig holes 6 to 12 inches apart and plant the plugs securely in the holes.

PROBLEM SOLVING

If you're unhappy with the condition of your lawn, chances are that at least one of the big three lawn spoilers—weeds, insects, and diseases—is responsible. Turfgrass makes few demands, but when confronted by less than ideal conditions—shade, slopes, poor drainage, and poor care—those unwelcome pests quickly move in.

Your first instinct likely may be to do something to control the pests, and you can certainly do that. But it's also important to recognize that weeds, insects, and diseases are often signs that something else is wrong: in your lawn, under it, or with its maintenance program. Rather than cursing the symptoms and treating them with after-the-fact, quick-fix solutions, look at them as an opportunity to get at the root of the problem. And remember, if you don't resolve the underlying cause, you will probably face the problem over and over again.

So, before investing in chemical solutions, take a good hard look at the kind of care you're giving your lawn, the environment in which you want it to grow, the suitability of the grass for your climate, and its tolerance to common diseases and insects in your area. Here's a sampling of what can go wrong and some possible solutions.

POOR DRAINAGE: When water stands on the lawn or saturates the soil, grass struggles. Moisture-loving weeds, such as ground ivy and speedwell, move in and pythium blight and other diseases thrive. If the problem is minor, simply aerating may solve it. But if drainage problems are serious and persistent, you may need to regrade the area or install drainage tiles to funnel water away.

POOR WATERING: Overwatering is as bad as poor drainage. Watering too frequently weakens plant roots, which provides an entrance for many diseases. Although underwatering can stress turf, most grasses will go dormant when water is scarce.

SLOPES: Soil drains irregularly on steep slopes. It may be too dry at the top and too wet at the bottom. Sloping turf also is difficult to mow, fertilize, and water properly. That's why slopes often have more weeds than level

Poor drainage

Shade

Traffic

Poor mowing

Slope

Poor watering

HEALTHY LAWN REGIME

■ Grow the proper grass for your climate and conditions.
■ Test the soil for nutrients and pH annually and correct as necessary.
■ Check soil for compaction at various locations throughout the yard.
■ Aerate every year or two and topdress afterward with topsoil, shredded compost, or sand.
■ Check for thatch annually. Remove if it is more than ½ inch thick.
■ Trim or remove trees and shrubs to reduce shade and increase air flow.
■ Fertilize lightly at the correct time for your area (see page 34).
■ Mow lightly and regularly. Do not let the grass exceed its maximum recommended height (page 41) by more than a third.
■ Water infrequently but deeply. When irrigating, run sprinklers long enough to put down 1 inch of water. Make sure the water soaks into the soil rather than runs off.
■ Inspect the grass at least once a month: Get down on your hands and knees to look for insects, diseases, and weeds. If you find them, take appropriate action as described on the following pages.

ground. If regrading is not an option, consider replacing the turf with a hardy ground cover such as crown vetch.

SHADE: Most turfgrasses are sun lovers. Shade slows their growth—blades become spindly and the turf thins out—and weeds and diseases get the upper hand. However, it's not impossible to grow grass in shade. First, some species—most notably fine fescue, St. Augustinegrass, and zoysiagrass—are shade tolerant. Next, you can reduce the amount of shade by trimming trees, and by mowing higher, fertilizing less, and watering deeply, you can help the grass withstand the shade.

POOR MOWING: Mowing too low and too infrequently are common causes of disease and weed infestations because they weaken the grass. Also, the turf thins out under this kind of care, and any empty spot in the lawn is an open invitation to weeds. To forestall weed and disease invasion, follow the correct mowing schedule for your grass.

TRAFFIC: High-traffic areas where you walk, play ball, or barbecue are perfect spots for weeds. Many weeds are much better adapted than turfgrasses to the compacted soil that comes with heavy use. And as the turf thins under the traffic, the open spots offer places for the weeds to move in. Consider planting a wear-resistant grass that won't thin out. Or replace the turf with hardscaping such as paving blocks or bricks.

WEEDS

Perhaps nowhere else is the classic definition of weeds—plants out of place—more appropriate than in the lawn. Ideally, no plant has a place in the lawn except turfgrass, but keeping the turf totally weed free is impossible. There will always be weeds cropping up, and it's up to you to decide how many you can abide. Weeds are not a monolithic enemy. Some are more tolerable than others. The more you're willing to put up with, the easier your job will be.

Much like turfgrasses, weeds fall into different categories defined by their physical characteristics and growth habits. Learning about their lifestyles can offer some important clues for controlling them.

First, weeds may be classified as annual, biennial, or perennial. Annual weeds, such as crabgrass, reproduce by seed and live out their entire lives in one year. Removing these weeds before seed forms will go a long way toward controlling the following year's crop.

Biennial weeds, such as mallow, live for two years. Usually the first year's growth is strictly vegetative. The plants don't set seed until the second year. They may reproduce by seed or vegetative means. So, for best control you must kill or remove the crown and root as well as the seeds.

Perennial weeds live year after year. Many, such as bermudagrass, produce seeds but mainly reproduce vegetatively. With these, each underground rhizome or aboveground stolon can develop its own roots and leaves and become a separate plant, especially after breaking off from the parent plant. To control such weeds, you must kill or remove all stolons, rhizomes, and roots before seeds form.

Both annual and perennial weeds may also be classified as either cool- or warm-season, depending on the conditions in which they grow best. Cool-season weeds thrive in the

Henbit, a cool season weed, appears early in the spring.

Because quack grass is a grassy weed, applying postemergence herbicides to control it may also harm turf.

mild temperatures of early spring and autumn; warm-season weeds are at their best in the heat of summer. They can be especially troublesome in northern lawns because they grow vigorously at the same time the cool-

Dandelion is a broadleaf weed with growth characteristics much different than turfgrasses.

MOWING AND WEEDS

Though we rarely think of it in these terms, the lawn mower can be a valuable weed control tool if used properly. Studies have shown that high mowing can help to reduce weed populations. One study showed that in a lawn mowed at 2¼ inches, crabgrass cover was reduced from 30 percent to 7 percent in five years. That compares favorably to a plot mowed at 1¼ inches in which crabgrass cover increased from 30 to 33 percent after five years.

High mowing works to retard the growth of many annual weeds. The principle is simple: The taller grass helps to shade and cool the soil and restricts the germination of annual weeds.

If annual weeds do take hold, the lawn mower can help to control their spread. Mowing regularly so seed heads do not develop will prevent weed seeds from becoming established.

Purslane is most troublesome in summer when turf is stressed by heat and drought.

season grasses are stressed by heat. In the South, they thrive under summer schedules of watering and feeding. When warm-season weeds are a problem in either area, keep watering and fertilizing to a minimum.

Finally, weeds are classified as either broadleaf or grassy (narrow leaf). This is an important distinction to remember when using herbicides. Most herbicides labeled to control broadleaf weeds won't control grassy weeds, and vice versa.

Herbicides can be preemergent or postemergence (some are used both ways) and nonselective or selective. Preemergence herbicides kill plants before they emerge from the soil. Postemergence herbicides work after plants start to grow. Nonselective herbicides are toxic to all plant life and are often used to kill an entire lawn before replanting.

A selective herbicide will kill one weed but not another, but be cautious. An herbicide labeled to kill grassy weeds could kill the turf, too. Always read herbicide labels completely before using them. Be sure the product is labeled as effective against the weed and is safe for the specific grass or cultivar you're growing. And follow the guidelines for timing the applications.

All in all, there are many ways to control weeds: You can pull them, cut them, shade them, mow them, even burn them, or you can kill them with chemicals. Some of these remedies offer a quick fix; others take time and patience. The rogues' gallery of weeds on the following pages provides information for controlling many of the turf weeds, with broadleaf types first, and then grassy weeds.

WEEDING TOOLS

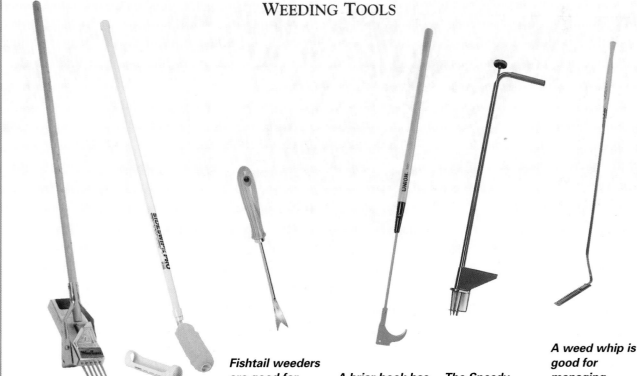

Weed Poppers® feature spring-loaded teeth that you jam into the turf under the roots of weeds. Stomp on the foot petal to extract the weeds.

Use a weed swiper like a paint roller to apply contact herbicides directly to weeds. The swiper helps avoid getting herbicides on the turfgrass.

Fishtail weeders are good for cutting off the taproots of weeds deep below the surface, which helps prevent weeds from resprouting. Long- and short-handled models are available.

A briar hook has a sharp, hooked end that you use to pry weeds with strong taproots, such as dandelions, from the lawn. It is especially good for weeding sidewalk cracks.

The Speedy Weedy extricates tough weeds from the lawn without damaging surrounding turf. Insert the metal fingers into the turf around the weed, twist, and pull.

A weed whip is good for managing rough low-maintenance areas where lawn mowers aren't practical. Swing it by the handle and slice off even the tallest and toughest of weeds and grasses.

WEEDS
continued

Black medic thrives in dry soils and spotty turf.

Black Medic
Medicago lupulina

Annual, broadleaf (sometimes survives as a short-lived perennial)
RANGE: Throughout the United States.
APPEARANCE: With its three-leaflet, cloverlike leaves, this legume is often confused with white clover. Low growing, with trailing, slightly hairy stems, it produces clusters of small, bright yellow flowers in late spring to early summer.
GROWTH: Black medic is common in lawns from May through September. It is especially prevalent in dry soils where turf is spotty and in high-phosphorus soils. Though an annual, black medic can be as persistent as a perennial.
CHEMICAL CONTROLS: Apply a postemergence broadleaf herbicide containing triclopyr, or mecoprop + 2,4-D + dicamba, while plants are actively growing.
PHYSICAL CONTROLS: Keep lawn well watered to encourage thick turf. Maintain soil phosphorus in the low-to-medium range and ensure the lawn receives adequate nitrogen. Pull or dig the shallow taproots whenever the plants appear.

Broadleaf plantain first appears in midspring in thin turf.

Broadleaf Plantain
Plantago major

Perennial, broadleaf
RANGE: Throughout the United States and southern Canada.
APPEARANCE: Broadleaf plantain has gray-green, egg-shaped, wavy-edged leaves growing in ground-hugging rosettes. Narrow seed heads appear in a long cluster on a central, upright stem.
GROWTH: Rosettes appear in mid-spring in thin and weakened turf. Seed stalks rise from early summer through September. The rosette has a tendency to suffocate desirable lawn grasses.
  Plantain grows from seed and resprouting roots. Seed germinates best in rich, moist, compacted soil.
CHEMICAL CONTROLS: Spot treat with a postemergence herbicide containing triclopyr or mecoprop + 2,4-D + dicamba before flowers appear.
PHYSICAL CONTROLS: Proper turf maintenance helps discourage plantain. Collect clippings when mowing to keep from spreading seeds. Don't let flower spikes or seeds develop. Aerate the lawn. Dig up and dispose of young plants.

Curly dock arises from a fleshy taproot during hot, dry weather.

Curly Dock
Rumex crispus

Perennial, broadleaf
RANGE: Throughout the United States.
APPEARANCE: Bright, shiny green, lance-shaped leaves appear in spring. In summer and fall, the puckered wavy edges of the leaves are tinted reddish purple. Small greenish flowers appear on a tall, narrow spike that arises from the center of the plant.
GROWTH: Growing from a large, brownish taproot, curly dock is a perennial weed that grows most actively during the same period as when grass is suffering from the stress of hot, dry weather.
CHEMICAL CONTROLS: Spot treat individual curly dock plants with a postemergence herbicide containing triclopyr or triclopyr + clopyralid, or one with 2,4-D, or mecoprop + 2,4-D + dicamba.
PHYSICAL CONTROLS: Pull curly dock out by hand or dig it up with a small spade. Any pieces of the root left behind, though, will resprout.

Dandelion
Taraxacum officinale

Perennial, broadleaf
RANGE: Throughout the United States.
APPEARANCE: Everyone recognizes the bright yellow flowers of dandelions; they appear in early spring and are followed by puffy seed heads. They arise from rosettes of lance-shaped leaves.
GROWTH: Dandelions emerge in early spring, with flowering commencing as early as April and continuing through summer and fall. The plants reproduce from a long taproot, and from seeds. Seedlings can germinate at any time throughout the growing season.
CHEMICAL CONTROLS: Spot treat lawns with a postemergence herbicide containing triclopyr or one with mecoprop + 2,4-D + dicamba in summer through autumn. Corn meal glutin, an alternative herbicide, has been an effective preemergence control.
PHYSICAL CONTROLS: Remove grass clippings to prevent the spread of seeds. Dandelions thrive in weak, thin turf so water, mow, and fertilize correctly. Digging dandelions is successful only if you remove at least three-fourths of the root.

Dandelion readily sprouts from both taproots and seeds.

English Daisy

Bellis perennis

Perennial, broadleaf
RANGE: Northern half of the United States.
APPEARANCE: Leaves of this perennial vary from nearly smooth to hairy, and form an extremely dense cluster. The daisylike flowers growing on 2-inch stalks have bright yellow centers highlighted with white to pinkish outer rays.
GROWTH: English daisy has long since gone from an ornamental to a well-established and fast-growing lawn weed. It grows most rapidly in spring and fall and in all seasons on the West Coast, if protected from drought and heat.
CHEMICAL CONTROLS: Spot treat with postemergence herbicide containing mecoprop + 2,4-D + dicamba in spring.
PHYSICAL CONTROLS: Dig up the fleshy root. Once established, English daisy is difficult to control.

Almost too pretty to worry about, English daisy spreads rapidly.

Ground Ivy
Glechoma hederacea

Perennial, broadleaf
RANGE: Eastern half of the United States.
APPEARANCE: Also known as creeping charlie, this member of the mint family sports bright green, kidney-shaped leaves on hollow stems. Lavender flowers appear from early spring through summer.
GROWTH: Originally introduced as a ground cover for shady areas, this plant spreads rapidly by creeping stems that root at the nodes. It grows actively from early spring through fall, in sun and shade, as long as soil is damp. It does particularly well in poorly drained areas. Ground ivy reproduces from seed and its stems root easily upon soil contact.
CHEMICAL CONTROLS: Spot treat individual plants in spring and fall with a postemergence herbicide containing triclopyr, or one with mecoprop + 2,4-D + dicamba. Some researchers have used borax to rid lawns of ground ivy, however, it is a nonselective control.
PHYSICAL CONTROLS: Improve soil drainage; water turf sparingly. To remove existing plants, rake to raise the runners, then mow closely.

Ground ivy grows via creeping stems that root at the nodes.

WEEDS
continued

Henbit is one of the first weeds to appear in spring lawns.

Henbit
Lamium amplexicaule

Annual, broadleaf
RANGE: Entire United States.
APPEARANCE: Henbit, also known as dead nettle or bee nettle, has the typical square-shaped main stem of the mint family plants, of which it is a member. Rounded, toothed leaves grow to ½-inch diameter. Flowers are trumpet shaped and a pale purple in color.
GROWTH: This annual makes its first appearance in late winter or early spring. Its stems lie close to the ground, then curve and grow upright. The stems often root at lower nodes wherever they touch the soil. Henbit most frequently invades thin areas of lawns having rich soil.
CHEMICAL CONTROLS: Apply a preemergence herbicide containing pendimethalin before seeds germinate or use a postemergence herbicide with mecoprop + 2,4-D + dicamba after germination in spring or fall. Do not water the lawn for 24 hours afterward.
PHYSICAL CONTROLS: Henbit is shallow rooted and easy to pull from the lawn. Around trees and shrubs, you can keep henbit in control with generous mulching.

Mouse-ear chickweed is a problem especially in moist, shady areas.

Mouse-Ear Chickweed
Cerastium fontanum vulgare

Annual or perennial, broadleaf
RANGE: Throughout the United States.
APPEARANCE: The name of this weed offers a clue to its appearance. It has long, narrow, fleshy leaves that look fuzzy. Small, white flowers appear in late spring and early summer, followed by seed heads in midsummer.
GROWTH: This weed grows most actively during spring and early summer, when it spreads by means of creeping stems that root at the nodes. Because it grows close to the ground, it withstands low mowing. It grows vigorously in moist, poorly drained, and shaded areas.
CHEMICAL CONTROLS: Apply postemergence herbicides containing triclopyr or mecoprop + 2,4-D + dicamba to young plants in spring before they go to seed.
PHYSICAL CONTROLS: In early spring, rake vigorously to raise the runners, then cut them off either by hand or with a mower set very low. Overseed thinning turfgrasses with improved varieties, especially in shaded areas.

Prostrate knotweed can be identified by its nonrooting, spreading stems.

Prostrate Knotweed
Polygonum aviculare

Annual, broadleaf
RANGE: Throughout the United States.
APPEARANCE: Characterized by tough, wiry stems that radiate from a central taproot, prostrate knotweed forms a mat of foliage with blue-green, oblong leaves. Tiny white flowers appear at the junction of leaf and stem.
GROWTH: Propagation is by seed. The spreading stems do not root, however the plants are deep rooted. Seedlings emerge in late winter to early spring, when the first warm temperatures arrive. The young growth often is mistaken for grass. This weed often appears in hard, compacted soils, such as heavily trafficked areas and along sidewalks and driveways.
CHEMICAL CONTROLS: Apply a postemergence herbicide containing mecoprop + 2,4-D + dicamba from mid- to late spring when the weed is young. It should have only three to four ranks of leaves up its stem.
PHYSICAL CONTROLS: Aerate the turf to correct compacted soil conditions.

Prostrate Spurge And Spotted Spurge

Euphorbia supina **and** *E. maculata*

Annual, broadleaf
RANGE: Eastern two-thirds of the United States as well as the Pacific Northwest coast.
APPEARANCE: Both of these weeds grow in rosettes, with stems radiating from a central point. Small, oblong leaves have a purple tint. Spotted spurge flowers are pinkish white and inconspicuous.

GROWTH: The spreading branches of these annuals choke out desirable grasses. Plants bloom throughout summer, and set seed in late summer and fall. Seed germinates when soil temperatures reach 60° F. Spurge is most often a problem in thin, undernourished turf subject to drought stress.
CHEMICAL CONTROLS: Apply preemergence herbicide containing pendimethalin or balan in late spring before seeds germinate. Or apply a postemergence herbicide containing triclopyr after plants begin growth.
PHYSICAL CONTROLS: Keep turf irrigated, do not fertilize in summer.

The spurges can be recognized by their purple-tinted, oblong leaves.

Puncturevine

Tribulus terrestris

Annual, broadleaf
RANGE: Throughout the United States except the far North.
APPEARANCE: Low, branching, creeping plant with 2-inch-long hairy, pale, glossy green leaves, divided into five to seven pairs. The hairs can give the plant a silvery appearance. Pale yellow flowers appear from July to September, followed by seed heads with thorny seedpods; these are prickly and are often carried on clothes and pets.

GROWTH: Also called devil's weed, puncturevine germinates in summer and produces a deep, central taproot. Each plant may spread up to 5 feet across. Puncturevine thrives in infertile, compacted soil.
CHEMICAL CONTROLS: Spot treat with a postemergent containing mecoprop + 2,4-D + dicamba during active growth.
PHYSICAL CONTROLS: Aerate the soil to reduce compaction.

Puncturevine is a prostrate plant with yellow flowers and stickers.

Purslane

Portulaca oleracea

Annual, broadleaf
RANGE: Throughout the United States, especially troublesome east of the Mississippi River.
APPEARANCE: Sprawling, thick, fleshy stems with rubbery leaves. Tiny, yellow, five-petaled flowers open when the sun is shining brightly. Cup-shaped seedpods produce many small, black seeds that may lie dormant in the soil for years. Purslane is seldom found in the spring when the lawn is treated for other weeds.

GROWTH: It thrives in hot, dry weather, spreading by sprawling stems. It's extremely troublesome in thin areas of the lawn or in new lawns seeded in summer.
CHEMICAL CONTROLS: Apply preemergence herbicides containing pendimethalin or balan. Or from mid- to late summer, spot treat with a postemergence herbicide containing triclopyr or mecoprop + 2,4-D + dicamba. If you have just reseeded the lawn, wait until after three mowings before treating.
PHYSICAL CONTROLS: Maintain dense turf. When planting a lawn in summer, let the area lie fallow before seeding.

Purslane is a problem in dry, spotty turf and in new lawns.

WEEDS
continued

Speedwell produces violetlike white or purple flowers.

Speedwell
Veronica officinalis

Perennial or annual, broadleaf
RANGE: Eastern half of the northeastern United States, except in the extreme South.
APPEARANCE: There are several types of speedwell, all characterized by small, lobed, and numerous leaves, and by tiny white or purple flowers. The scallop-edged leaves are paired, growing opposite each other. Heart-shaped seed pods grow on the stems below the flowers.
GROWTH: Speedwells are among the earliest of lawn weeds to appear, greening up as early as late winter. Most are characterized by creeping stems that root at the nodes. Some show an erect growth habit as they mature. They all thrive in cool, moist soils where turf has thinned.
CHEMICAL CONTROLS: Apply a preemergence herbicide containing pendimethalin, balan, or dacthal before seeds germinate. Treat with a postemergence herbicide containing triclopyr or one with mecoprop + 2,4-D + dicamba when plants are flowering or actively growing.
PHYSICAL CONTROLS: Fertilize cool-season lawns in fall instead of in spring. Improve soil drainage.

White clover grows in early spring, and browns out in late summer.

White Clover
Trifolium repens

Perennial, broadleaf
RANGE: Northern half of the United States.
APPEARANCE: Once regularly included as an ingredient in lawn seed mixes, low-growing white clover is characterized by its three-part leaves and white blossoms resembling pom-poms. Though it may be considered attractive, it enters dormancy early in the fall and during periods of drought, leaving unsightly brown patches in the lawn.
GROWTH: White clover emerges from dormancy in early spring and spreads by aggressive above- and below-ground stems. It also reproduces by seeds. It continues to grow into the fall, as long as moisture levels are adequate. White clover is especially aggressive in high-phosphorus soils.
CHEMICAL CONTROLS: In fall, apply a postemergence herbicide that contains either triclopyr or mecoprop + 2,4-D + dicamba. Spray while plants are actively growing on warm, but not hot, windless days.

Yellow wood sorrel looks like a yellow-flowered clover.

Yellow Wood Sorrel
Oxalis stricta

Annual or perennial, broadleaf
RANGE: Throughout the United States.
APPEARANCE: Oxalis closely resembles clover with its three-part, heart-shaped leaflets. As flowers mature, cucumber-shaped light green seedpods take their place. When pods are completely dry, the slightest touch will send its seeds scattering for several feet in all directions.
GROWTH: Yellow wood sorrel grows most vigorously in spring and late summer to fall, especially in moist, fertile soils. This upright annual (which sometimes acts like a perennial) sends out roots from its lower nodes.
CHEMICAL CONTROLS: Spot treat in spring or late summer to fall with a postemergence herbicide containing triclopyr or mecoprop + 2,4-D + dicamba, when the weeds are actively growing. Several treatments are usually needed.
PHYSICAL CONTROLS: Keeping the lawn healthy helps to control oxalis by crowding it out. Plants are relatively easy to pull by hand.

Annual Bluegrass
Poa annua

Annual, grassy
RANGE: Throughout the United States. Considered a winter annual in the South, where it's often used for overseeding.
APPEARANCE: Fine, green blades, growing in a creeping habit; seed heads, evident at a low height, rise above the grass, giving the lawn a whitish appearance.
GROWTH: Annual bluegrass germinates early in spring or late fall, but tends to die out in summer, leaving bare patches in the lawn.

Seeds continue to form even under extremely close mowing. This weed is usually found in cool, frequently watered areas, shaded sections of turf, and lawns with compacted soil.
CHEMICAL CONTROLS: Apply a preemergence herbicide containing pendimethalin or benefin in early spring or late summer before seeds germinate. Or for small patches, make postemergence applications of fluazifop, which is a nonselective grass killer.
PHYSICAL CONTROLS: Increase mowing height and remove clippings when seed heads are present. Aerate to reduce soil compaction.

Annual bluegrass grows vigorously in spring, but dies out in summer.

Dallisgrass
Paspalum dilatatum

Perennial, grassy
RANGE: Coastal states from New Jersey to California, and as far north as Missouri.
APPEARANCE: Coarse blades, somewhat upright in a bunch-type growth. Rhizomes are so closely jointed that they appear almost scaly. Stems 2 to 6 inches long emerge from the plant center in a starlike pattern. Seed heads are sparsely branched on long stems. Seeds lie dormant over the winter and sprout very early in spring.

GROWTH: This is a summer weed in many areas of the country, but it grows throughout the year in mild climates and thrives in those areas that are low and wet.
CHEMICAL CONTROLS: Spot treat with a postemergence herbicide containing fluazifop, which is a nonselective grass killer, or calcium acid methanearsonate in spring or early summer.
PHYSICAL CONTROLS: Avoid spring fertilization and overwatering. Find methods of draining soil to control dallisgrass in moist areas. Digging up clumps can be difficult because dallisgrass has deep roots.

Dallisgrass is a southern perennial that thrives in dry soil.

Green Foxtail
Setaria viridis

Annual, grassy
RANGE: Throughout the United States, especially cooler regions, and in parts of Canada.
APPEARANCE: Often called bristlegrass and sometimes mistaken for crabgrass, green foxtail is a semierect bunch grass. It often has a reddish tint and grows 1 to 2 feet tall. The seed heads are dense and bristly. The seeds sprout from midspring to early summer.
GROWTH: Seeds germinate when soil temperature reaches 65° F;

plants grow vigorously through summer. Foxtail dies with the first killing frost. Growth is most vigorous in closely mowed, thin turf that is watered and fertilized frequently in summer.
CHEMICAL CONTROLS: Apply a preemergence herbicide containing benefin or pendimethalin before seeds germinate. Or spot treat small patches with fluazifop, which is a nonselective grass killer, or calcium acid methanearsonate when plants are actively growing.
PHYSICAL CONTROLS: Remove grass clippings when foxtail seed heads are present; aerate soil.

Green foxtail is an semierect warm-season annual grass.

WEEDS
continued

Nimblewill is a creeping grass that dies early in the season (main photo).

Nimblewill
Muhlenbergia schreiberi

Perennial, grassy
RANGE: Eastern and central United States.
APPEARANCE: With fine, blue-green to light green blades, and a creeping habit, nimblewill resembles creeping bentgrass. However, its leaves are slow to color in the spring, resulting in straw-colored lawn patches early in the season in nimblewill-infested lawns. Wiry stems grow up to 10 inches tall—first outward and then upward from the central crown.

GROWTH: Nimblewill thrives in hot, dry conditions and thin, drought-stressed turf. It emerges in summer and continues growing until the first killing frost. Stems root at lower nodes as the plants reach out.
CHEMICAL CONTROLS: Spot treat small areas with a postemergence herbicide containing fluazifop, which is a nonselective grass killer. Begin control in early spring because nimblewill is easiest to eliminate when it's a seedling.
PHYSICAL CONTROLS: Avoid fertilizing the lawn in summer. Dig or pull out plants while they are still seedlings.

Quackgrass
Agropyron repens

Perennial, grassy
RANGE: Throughout the United States except in the extreme South.
APPEARANCE: Quackgrass is characterized by light green to blue-green coarse blades that are rough on their upper surface. In unmowed areas, it can grow to 3 feet tall. Roots can reach 5 feet deep or more in a single season. Narrow flower spikes rising from the plant resemble rye or wheat. The plant spreads by large, white rhizomes.

GROWTH: Quackgrass grows quickly in spring and fall. It is especially vigorous in thin, under-nourished turf. Though it sometimes goes unnoticed in early spring, quackgrass becomes quite obvious as it turns brown in summer.
CHEMICAL CONTROLS: Spot treat with a postemergence herbicide that contains fluazifop, which is a nonselective grass killer.
PHYSICAL CONTROLS: The spread of quackgrass can be checked to some degree by mowing low, cutting the runners, and maintaining dense turf. Hand digging is rarely successful.

Quackgrass is an invasive creeping grass that browns out in summer.

Crabgrass germinates late and dies with the first frost.

Smooth Crabgrass and Hairy Crabgrass

Digitaria ischaemum and *D. sanguinalis*

Annual, grassy
RANGE: Entire United States.
APPEARANCE: Smooth and hairy crabgrass have a prostrate growth habit with coarse, light green blades. The blades are short, pointed, and hairy.
GROWTH: This vigorous, warm-season annual grass grows rapidly from early spring until seed heads form in late summer to early fall. It grows especially well in thin turf or in lawns that are watered lightly, underfertilized, or poorly drained. Crabgrass spreads by seed.
CHEMICAL CONTROLS: Apply a preemergence herbicide containing pendimethalin, balan, or corn gluten meal before seeds germinate in spring. Or use a postemergent containing fluazifop, which is a nonselective grass killer, or calcium acid methanearsonate.
PHYSICAL CONTROLS: Maintain good management practices to grow thick, vigorous turf. Water deeply and use a high mowing height. Do not fertilize in summer.

Wild Onion and Wild Garlic

Allium canadense **and** A. *vineale*

Perennial, grassy
RANGE: Eastern and central states.
APPEARANCE: Wild onion and wild garlic are similar in habits but they are not the same plant. Both are characterized by clumps of smooth leaves, topped with small purple or white flowers in early summer. The stems of wild garlic are hollow; the stems of wild onion are not. Each plant has a characteristic onion scent.

GROWTH: Often the first to green up in the lawn, wild garlic and wild onion grow vigorously from early spring to midsummer, spreading by means of bulbs and roots. Wild garlic may also produce bulblets at its leaf tips. These bulblets can fall to the soil and sprout as they mature.
CHEMICAL CONTROLS: Spot treat with a postemergence herbicide containing mecoprop + 2,4-D + dicamba in late fall or early spring.
PHYSICAL CONTROLS: Mow at low heights in early spring to lessen any infestation; dig plants to remove bulbs and roots.

Wild garlic sprouts from small bulbs in early spring.

Yellow Nutsedge

Cyperus esculentus

Perennial, grassy
RANGE: Throughout the United States. A related species, purple nutsedge, is especially prevalent in the Southeast.
APPEARANCE: Though it resembles a grass, yellow nutsedge is actually a sedge. Its coarse, light green leaves grow upright from triangular stems. Seed heads appear from July to October.
GROWTH: Reproduces mainly from underground tubers; however, they can reproduce by seeds and underground stems. Tubers store food and are drought tolerant. Yellow nutsedge grows vigorously in summer, especially under moist conditions; primarily troublesome in closely mowed lawns.
CHEMICAL CONTROLS: Spot treat with calcium acid methanearsonate in late spring or early summer, as soon as the seed heads appear.
PHYSICAL CONTROLS: Mow high in early summer; water deep and infrequently. Hand pulling is not practical because any tubers left behind will sprout into new plants.

Yellow nutsedge thrives in moist soil, especially during summer.

Moss

There are hundreds of species of moss found in the United States. Though usually not classified as a weed, moss can be a problem in the home lawn.
RANGE: Throughout the United States.
APPEARANCE: Moss is a green, velvety, low-growing collection of plants that covers bare soil in shaded areas.
GROWTH: Mosses grow in moist situations, usually in the vicinity of trees. When moss appears, it is usually a good sign that the soil needs fertilizing. Moss usually appears in lawns as a result of poor drainage or poor air circulation, too much shade, or too little fertilizer.
CHEMICAL CONTROLS: Spray with ferrous sulfate or ferrous ammonium sulfate in early spring. Do not water after application. Surrounding lawn grass may darken for about a week.
PHYSICAL CONTROLS: Power rake the area vigorously to remove moss, and reseed with an improved grass variety. Also, reduce shade and improve air circulation by pruning nearby trees and shrubs; fertilize lawn on a regular basis.

Moss occurs in moist soil where turf is spotty.

INSECTS

There are hundreds of insect species living in and around your lawn. Chances are you never see most of them. In fact, the great majority of insects do little or no damage to the lawn; only a handful of them cause real harm.

For the best pest control, it's important to be able to recognize the bad guys, and familiarize yourself with their life cycles and habits. Good control depends on correct identification of the pest as well as a knowledge of its behavior, its biology, and the conditions that favor it.

Some pests thrive where it is warm and dry; others prefer cool or moist conditions. Other important factors that determine which types of pests you might encounter in your lawn

Insects that suck sap, such as this leafhopper, damage blades.

Mole crickets tunnel under turf, feeding on the grass roots.

include degree of shade or sunlight, amount of slope, and soil type.

If you suspect you have a pest problem, examine your lawn thoroughly to find the culprit. Pests are often found first in stressed areas—at the edge of the lawn, or in shady or wet areas. They are not usually distributed evenly throughout the lawn. Look for spots that have discolored, stunted, or distorted grass. Now take a closer look. Get down on

PEST-RESISTANT GRASSES

During the past several years, waging war against turf insects has become easier due to the introduction of pest-resistant grasses. These are varieties of perennial ryegrass and fescues that carry microscopic fungi known as endophytes. Endophytes repel a broad range of insects, some of which include greenbug, armyworm, billbug, cutworm, and sod webworm. Among the most pest-resistant grass varieties are: 'Repell', 'Citation II', 'Pennant', and 'Nobility' perennial ryegrasses, and 'Jamestown II', 'SR 3000', and 'Bridgeport' fescues.

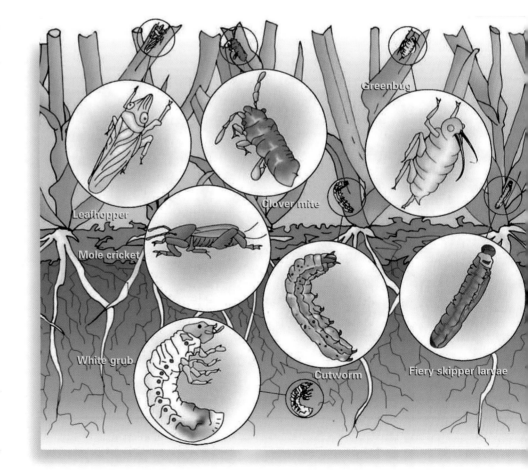

Leafhopper

Greenbug

Clover mite

Mole cricket

White grub

Cutworm

Fiery skipper larvae

your hands and knees, and concentrate your attention on the area of the damage. Insects tend to proceed outwards from a central point; therefore, they are generally most active on the outside edge.

Part the leaves of grass and look into the thatch layer. Focus on a specific area for several seconds and watch for insect movements. Look for evidence of pest infestation, such as the green, pellet-shaped droppings left by sod webworms.

If leafhopper, scale, or spider mites are at work, they can be found by examining the stems, leaves, and crowns of the plants. Chinch bugs live here, too, as well as in the thatch layer.

Other insects, such as sod webworms, can be driven to the surface of the soil by drenching a patch of lawn with pyrethrum, a natural pesticide. Mix 1 tablespoon of a 1- to 2-percent pyrethrum pesticide in 1 gallon of water. Mark off about 1 square yard, and apply the entire gallon mixture as evenly as possible using a sprinkling can. If those insects are present, within a few minutes they will rise to the surface of the lawn, where you can then spot and identify them.

Sod webworms feed on plants just above the thatch layer, leaving spots of dead, thin turf.

To hunt for grubs, cut and roll back a patch of sod and count the grubs in the soil. If you see more than six grubs per square foot, it's time to take action.

If you find insect pests, eradicate them according to the recommendations in the bug gallery on the following pages.

INSECTS

FEEDING ON BLADES:
Leafhopper
Clover mite
Greenbug
Billbug adult
Chinch bug

FEEDING ON CROWNS:
Cutworm
Fiery skipper larvae
Sod webworm larvae
Billbug larvae
Armyworm

FEEDING ON ROOTS:
White grub
Mole cricket
Ground pearl
Wireworm

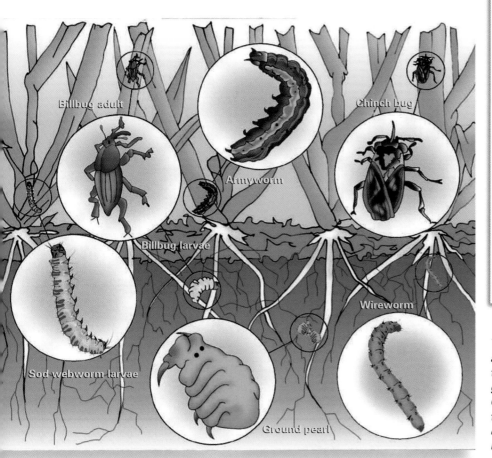

Turf pests live in, and damage, all areas of grass, from the blade tips to the crown to the roots. For example, greenbugs feed on the blades. Others, such as billbugs, live in the thatch. Japanese beetle grubs and other insects spend their lives underground feeding on the roots.

Armyworms are southern pests, especially on bermudagrass lawns.

Armyworms

SYMPTOMS: Small patches of brown turf with grass blades eaten off in circular patches to the soil surface. Tiny fuzz-covered eggs on the grass.

INSECT APPEARANCE: The armyworm caterpillars are light tan to dark brown with yellow, orange, or dark brown stripes down the lengths of their backs. They are ¾ inch to 2 inches long. Adult moths are tan or mottled gray with a wingspan of about 1 inch. They fly only at night or on overcast days. In daylight, they hide in the soil around grass roots.

LIFE CYCLE: Moths appear in late spring to early summer and lay hundreds of eggs at a time on the grass. Larvae hatch from eggs within 10 days and begin feeding. You may see the larvae hanging from threads on the grass. In the South, there may be as many as six generations a year.

DAMAGE THRESHOLD: More than five larvae per square yard indicates infestation.

CONTROLS: Acephate, *Bacillus thuringiensis* (Bt), carbaryl, cyfluthrin, neem, or pyrethrum.

Adult billbugs lay eggs in the stems of grass plants.

Billbugs

SYMPTOMS: A small and distinct circular pattern becomes yellowish or brown when billbugs are feeding on the lawn. Since the larvae feed on roots, grass plants within the dead areas easily lift out of the soil. A white sawdust-like debris can be found on the ground around the affected plants.

INSECT APPEARANCE: Billbug larvae—which do most of the damage—are white, legless grubs about ⅜ inch to ½ inch long. Brownish-gray adults have long snouts used for burrowing and chewing off plants.

LIFE CYCLE: Overwintering adults emerge in midspring, when they often can be found crawling on sidewalks and driveways. Soon after emerging, they lay eggs on the stems of grass plants. Grubs generally emerge in May or June and then tunnel into the stems, from where they eventually will migrate into the root zone.

DAMAGE THRESHOLD: More than one grub per square foot of lawn.

CONTROL: Spray grass foliage and thatch in spring (when the adult billbugs are moving around). Use carbaryl, cyfluthrin, or neem.

Black turfgrass ataenius grubs are very small larvae that consume grass roots.

Black Turfgrass Ataenius

SYMPTOMS: The larvae cause damage that appears similar to that inflicted by white grubs and Japanese beetles. Small patches of turf will begin to turn brown in late spring or early fall as the larvae hatch and feed. Afterwards, the dead patches of lawn roll back easily.

INSECT APPEARANCE: Adults are shiny, ¼-inch-long, black beetles Larvae are small grubs, less than one-fourth the size of other grubs; and white with brown heads.

LIFE CYCLE: Adults overwinter in the soil and emerge in spring when you'll see them flying during the hottest part of the day. They lay eggs in late spring, and then the larvae emerge soon afterward and begin feeding. There may be a second generation produced during late summer.

DAMAGE THRESHOLD: 30 to 40 grubs per square foot.

CONTROL: Carbaryl, cyfluthrin.

Chinch Bugs

SYMPTOMS: Large, distinct, circular yellowing patches that appear brown in the center, generally occurring only in sunny areas of the lawn.

INSECT APPEARANCE: Adult chinch bugs are small, from ¹⁄₁₆ to ¼ inch long, depending on the species. Most are black with white wings, each of which has a distinctive triangular black mark. Young chinch bugs are smaller, wingless versions of their parents, but are red with a white back stripe.

LIFE CYCLE: Adult chinch bugs overwinter in both the North and South and emerge as early as March. For the rest of the growing season, they feed by sucking the juice from grass blades, injecting a poison that causes blades to turn brown and die. They are especially active during hot, dry weather.

DAMAGE THRESHOLD: To find chinch bugs, push a bottomless 2-pound coffee can into the affected lawn area, about 2 inches deep. Fill it with warm water. Any chinch bugs present should float to the surface. If more than 20 chinch bugs appear, control is warranted.

CONTROL: Carbaryl, cyfluthrin. Reduce fertilization; plant resistant grass species.

Chinch bugs can also be recognized by their objectionable odor.

Crane Flies

SYMPTOMS: Beginning along the edges of the lawn, patches of turf brown out and die. Heavily infested areas show a brownish paste covering the soil where the grass has died.

INSECT APPEARANCE: The grubs (which do the damage) are brownish gray with a tough leathery texture. (Grubs are also called leatherjackets.) They are about an inch long and are usually found on top of, and just below, the soil surface. Adult crane flies resemble long-legged mosquitos, except they are much larger and do not bite.

LIFE CYCLE: Adults lay eggs in lawns in late summer; overwintering larvae emerge, and the grubs begin feeding on grass roots in early spring and continue to feed through summer.

DAMAGE THRESHOLD: Take action if you find more than five per square foot of lawn. Also look for a brownish paste covering the ground, which indicates a heavy infestation.

CONTROL: Beneficial nematodes, neem. Treatment is most effective in spring.

Adult crane flies produce root-eating larvae.

Cutworms

SYMPTOMS: As with armyworms, cutworms leave small, 1- to 2-inch-wide patches of brown grass in newly seeded and established lawns; the plants are eaten off at soil level.

INSECT APPEARANCE: The larvae of cutworms are plump, smooth, and almost always curl up when disturbed. They can be various colors but are most often gray, brown, or black; some are spotted or striped. They often grow to 2 inches long. The moths are dark and fly at night.

LIFE CYCLE: Moths lay their eggs in late summer, and after hatching, cutworm larvae overwinter in trash and clumps of grass. Larvae resume feeding early in spring (and only at night). They mature into moths in July or August.

DAMAGE THRESHOLD: Use the pyrethrum test (page 77), to determine how pervasive these insects are. If you find more than 10 larvae per square foot, it's time to act. Cutworms don't seriously damage grass unless there is a severe infestation. More damage may be done by birds scratching at the turf to feed on the larvae.

CONTROL: *Bacillus thuringiensis*, carbaryl, cyfluthrin, neem, pyrethrum.

Cutworms sometimes feed on grass blades.

INSECTS
continued

Fire ants ruin lawns with their massive mounds.

Fire Ants

SYMPTOMS: Large mounds of soil, 1 to 2 feet in diameter, and more than 1 foot high, appear throughout the lawn.

INSECT APPEARANCE: Ants are reddish in color and ¼ inch long or shorter. The head is normal size, but the last segment of the antenna is longer than that of other ants.

LIFE CYCLE: Most often a problem in sunny sites and clay soils in southern states.

DAMAGE THRESHOLD: Because fire ant mounds can destroy a lawn, and their bites are quite painful, just one mound is cause for action.

CONTROL: Acephate, bifenthrin, carbaryl, insecticidal soap. Drench the mound itself along with the area around the mound to a distance of 4 feet out.

Grasshoppers are turf pests only in severe drought.

Grasshoppers

SYMPTOMS: Grass plants chewed down to the crown.

INSECT APPEARANCE: Various species range from brown to yellow to green in color, and vary in size from 1 to 2 inches in length. They are all characterized by long bodies, large hind legs for jumping, and prominent jaws. Young grasshoppers lack fully developed wings.

LIFE CYCLE: Females lay eggs from midsummer into the autumn. Eggs hatch from late winter to late summer, depending on the climate. After the young nymphs molt, they begin feeding, and if food supplies grow scarce, they march across the countryside devouring all greenery in their path.

DAMAGE THRESHOLD: Grasshoppers are generally not a problem on the lawn unless large swarms of them move in to eat. This may happen in rural areas during dry weather, when the insects' normal food sources are nonexistent.

CONTROL: Treat with carbaryl, chlorpyrifos, *nosema locustae* bait, or pyrethrum when grasshoppers are young. If the number of grasshoppers is small, hand pick them early in the morning when they move more slowly.

Greenbugs may feed on grass blades in summer.

Greenbugs

SYMPTOMS: Rust-colored patches of grass appear under trees when greenbugs are feeding. These patches of grass turn brown and die as the insects continue to feed. The damage then spreads to sunny parts of the lawn. Grass blades may have yellow, rust-colored spots with dark centers. Underwatered or overfertilized Kentucky bluegrass lawns are particularly susceptible to this insect. Damage usually occurs after mild winters and cool springs.

INSECT APPEARANCE: A type of aphid, greenbugs are small, light green, and wedge shaped.

LIFE CYCLE: Greenbugs begin feeding in late spring and continue throughout the summer, producing many generations of the bugs. They basically suck sap from—and inject a poison into—grass blades as they feed on them.

DAMAGE THRESHOLD: Most times, greenbugs rarely build up to populations large enough to do damage to the lawn. However, if you sweep your hand over the grass and see greenbugs scatter, that indicates enough of a population to take action.

CONTROL: Treat with acephate or use an insecticidal soap.

Leafhoppers

SYMPTOMS: Areas of the lawn look pale or even white, and small white spots appear on individual blades of grass as leafhoppers suck the sap from them. Like aphids, they produce a sticky substance called honeydew. Grass also has a stunted, thinned appearance.

INSECT APPEARANCE: Tiny, less than 1/8 inch long even when fully grown, leafhoppers are wedge-shaped and pale green or yellow or gray. They fly or hop from blade to blade. Immature leafhoppers resemble the adults but are paler and wingless.

LIFE CYCLE: Adults overwinter in debris, emerge in midspring, and begin feeding. Females lay eggs in early summer, and within two weeks, nymphs emerge and begin feeding. In the northern states, only one generation appears yearly. There may be more than three generations in southern states.

DAMAGE THRESHOLD: Leafhoppers are nearly always present in lawns, but no action need be taken unless there is a severe infestation. If you kick up a swarm of leafhoppers with each step across the lawn, it's time to take action.

CONTROL: Acephate, carbaryl.

Leafhoppers are tiny insects that suck sap from grass blades.

Mites

SYMPTOMS: Patches of pale yellow, straw-colored, or silvery grass; thin, browned-out turf.

INSECT APPEARANCE: Microscopic mites are virtually impossible to spot without magnification. Mites have eight legs and are insect related rather than true insects. Clover mites are 1/30 inch long and green to red in color; bermudagrass mites are even smaller. They feed on the underside of grass blades. You may, however, see their fine webbing on the plants.

LIFE CYCLE: Mites are most active during hot, dry weather; they may overwinter in thatch or other protected areas.

DAMAGE THRESHOLD: Though they may be present on the lawn, mites rarely reach numbers high enough to cause problems. More than 1,000 per square foot is a serious infestation. Mites do the most damage in times of water stress.

CONTROL: Bifenthrin, insecticidal soap. Adequate watering helps to keep down spider mite populations.

Mites can be recognized by the presence of webs on grass blades.

Mole Crickets

SYMPTOMS: Irregular streaks of brown and wilted grass. The dead grass pulls up easily, and you can find the crickets' tunnels with your fingers or sometimes even see them, if the ground is bare. The lawn feels spongy underfoot.

INSECT APPEARANCE: Mole crickets are about 1½ to 2 inches long and brown or grayish brown. They look similar to the common cricket, except that their heads are large, and they have notable short, fat front legs.

LIFE CYCLE: Mole crickets are problems primarily in the Atlantic and Gulf Coast states. Adult crickets eat grass roots, and their nighttime tunneling—6 to 8 inches below the soil surface—damages roots and causes the soil to dry out beneath the lawn. Adult crickets emerge from the soil in the spring to mate.

DAMAGE THRESHOLD: More than two mole crickets per square foot of sod indicates it's time to begin treatment.

CONTROL: Acephate, beneficial nematodes, carbaryl, cyfluthrin, neem, or pyrethrum. Apply in spring about a week after the first signs of mole cricket activity appear.

Mole crickets do most of their damage by burrowing under turf.

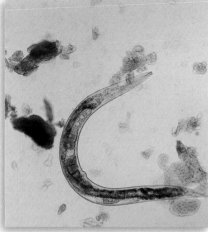

Nematodes are microscopic worms that feed on grass roots.

Nematodes

SYMPTOMS: Signs of nematode trouble are often subtle. They include slow-growing grass that is thin and yellowish and susceptible to summer drought. If you examine the grass roots, they may appear stubby and shallow, possibly showing galls.

INSECT APPEARANCE: These pests are invisible to the naked eye. Identifying them requires laboratory analysis by a professional.

LIFE CYCLE: Among the most plentiful life forms on earth, nematodes exist primarily in soil moisture and soil debris. Traveling very slowly through the soil, they attach themselves to plant roots. They suck juice from the plant and inject a chemical that causes galls to form.

DAMAGE THRESHOLD: Determined by nematode type, soil type, and climate; professional analysis needed.

CONTROL: Keep grass as healthy as possible. If presence of damaging nematodes is confirmed, use ethoprop. Fumigation of the soil before planting a new lawn is recommended, especially in the South where nematodes are more prevalent. Soils high in organic matter resist nematode infestation.

Rhodesgrass scale attacks St. Augustinegrass near its crown.

Scale Insects

SYMPTOMS: In late summer, grass turns brown and dies in irregular patches.

INSECT APPEARANCE: These tiny ¹⁄₁₆ to ⅛ inch long legless insects are covered with a hard, white shell. Bermudagrass scale can be found clinging to stems, while scale insects known as ground pearls attach themselves to roots. They look like bumps on leaves and roots.

LIFE CYCLE: These insects feed on the stems and roots of bermudagrass and centipedegrass, mostly in the South and Southwest. In warm climates, they can be active for as long as the grass is growing. They are especially prevalent in sandy soils.

DAMAGE THRESHOLD: If scale-caused brown patches spread throughout the lawn, or if stems are covered by scales, treatment may be required.

CONTROL: Drench with insecticidal soap; keep lawn well fertilized, watered, and mowed.

Sod webworm adults (right) lay eggs in turf, where the larvae hatch and feed.

Sod Webworms

SYMPTOMS: Dead patches from 1- to 2-inches wide, with grass blades chewed off just above the thatch line. Usually prevalent in the hottest, driest areas of the lawn. Silky white tubes found nestled in the root area.

INSECT APPEARANCE: Sod webworm larvae are slender, grayish, black-spotted caterpillars, approximately ¾ inch long, and sluggish in their activity. They hide during the day in shelters constructed of bits of grass and debris. The buff-colored moths, which fly in zigzag patterns over the lawn at dusk, have two snout-like projections on their heads.

LIFE CYCLE: Overwintering larvae emerge and begin feeding (at night or on overcast days) in spring. They mature into moths in early summer. Throughout the summer, the moths fly over the grass and drop eggs, which hatch into larvae and repeat the feeding cycle on the grass. There may be as many as three generations per season.

DAMAGE THRESHOLD: Fifteen or more larvae per square foot indicates treatment is necessary.

CONTROL: Acephate, Bt, carbaryl, neem, pyrethrum; plant resistant grasses.

White Grubs

SYMPTOMS: Irregularly shaped brown patches of turf, particularly in late spring or early fall. Dead patches of lawn roll back easily, like a section of carpet. Birds, moles, raccoons, and skunks may damage a lawn looking for grubs.

INSECT APPEARANCE: White grubs have curled C-shaped bodies from ¼ to ¾ inches long. They are creamy white with yellow or brown heads and dark hind parts. Adults vary in appearance because white grubs are the larvae of scarab beetles, June bugs, rose chafers, Asiatic beetles, and others.

LIFE CYCLE: Grubs overwinter and begin feeding early in spring. Adult beetles appear around late spring or early summer. A second generation emerges in late summer and feeds in autumn.

DAMAGE THRESHOLD: Cut and lift a 1-square-foot section of sod. If more than six white grubs are present in the soil, it's time to apply a treatment.

CONTROL: Beneficial nematodes, carbaryl, halofenozide, or neem. Repeated heavy waterings are needed after application to carry pesticides down through the grass and thatch into the soil level where most of the grubs live.

White grubs feed primarily on the roots of cool-season grasses.

Wireworms

SYMPTOMS: Wireworm damage to the lawn resembles grub damage: Irregular patches of turf turn brown and die. Dead sod is easily lifted from the soil.

INSECT APPEARANCE: The larvae of click beetles, wireworms are brown, hard-shelled worms that grow to about 1½ inches in length. The adult beetles are ½ to ¾ inch long with flattened, dark brown bodies, often with darker markings.

LIFE CYCLE: Wireworms overwinter as adult beetles or pupae. In spring, beetles lay eggs in sod; larvae emerge soon after and begin feeding on plant roots. These insects, which remain as feeding larvae for two to six years, are most often found in moist soils.

DAMAGE THRESHOLD: To check for wireworms, bury whole potatoes about 3 inches deep in various 3-inch-wide locations around the lawn. If, after three or four days, the potatoes are crawling with wireworms, it's time to take action. (Be sure to destroy the potatoes; do not compost.)

CONTROL: Have a professional treat the soil before seeding the lawn to prevent the insects from destroying seedlings.

Wireworms are the hard-shelled larvae of click beetles.

Moles and Gophers

Moles and gophers are rodents that live underground. Moles feed on earthworms, grubs, and other insects; gophers eat plant roots or entire plants. Each causes damage to the lawn by severing grass roots, raising sod, and in the case of gophers, eating sections of the lawn.

Moles are 6 to 8 inches long with gray to black velvety fur. Gophers are brown, with small eyes and ears and conspicuous pouches on either sides of their mouths. When moles are present, you will notice raised ridges, 3 to 5 inches wide, that crisscross the lawn. These ridges sometimes turn brown because the tunnels have destroyed the grass roots. Gophers create crescent-shaped mounds of soil on the lawn. On close probing, you will find a hole underneath each mound. Gophers usually are found in the western United States.

Trapping or baiting is the best way to eliminate gophers from your yard. Moles are harder to control with traps or poisons because of the fragile, temporary nature of their tunnels. The best way to help rid your lawn of moles is to eliminate their favorite food—grubs.

Moles damage lawns as they search for insects on which to feed.

DISEASES

Topdress to retard disease development.

Turf diseases may appear as circular or irregularly shaped patches of dead or brown grass (top), or as spots on individual blades of grass (above).

Virtually all turf diseases are caused by soil-dwelling fungi. Normally these pathogens are held in check by beneficial fungi and other microorganisms. It is only when conditions become favorable for the pathogens that they gain the upper hand and do their dirty work on the grass.

Improper management is the main cause for most of the diseases that attack home lawns. Turf diseases can be controlled with fungicides, but your first action should be to understand the conditions that give rise to disease, then correct them so diseases won't get started in the first place. Here are the primary cultural and environmental culprits that allow disease to gain a foothold in the lawn.

EXCESSIVE FERTILIZER: Too much fertilizer may acidify the soil and create conditions that favor pathogens over other soil organisms. However, the main problems from excessive fertilization arise because it makes the grass grow too fast. The grass becomes lush and succulent and thus easy prey for disease organisms. In some grasses, too much fertilizer may also encourage thatch, which not only harbors disease-causing organisms but also weakens the grass by slowing the passage of water and nutrients. If you inspect your grass and your thatch is thicker than ½ inch, it could be causing problems. To help prevent disease, apply fertilizer in the right amount at the right times for your lawn.

EXCESSIVE PESTICIDE USE: Relying on pesticides to solve all the problems in your yard creates a vicious cycle. Fungicides, insecticides, and herbicides greatly decrease the microorganism population in the soil, destroying beneficial microorganisms as well as harmful ones. When faced with disease and other problems, it's understandable that you reach for the quick-fix solution. But before spraying anything, be sure to identify the culprit, then match the solution to the problem. In this way you can cut down on your chemical usage.

IMPROPER WATERING: Some diseases like wet roots; others multiply rapidly on moist leaves. Be careful of excessive watering or repeated light sprinkling. To stall the advance

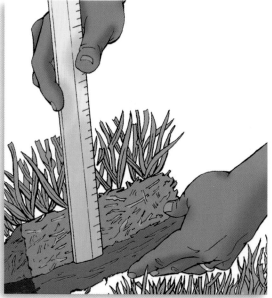

A thick thatch layer can lead to diseased turf.

Replace grass in heavy shade.

The following pages list the most common diseases of turfgrass, including symptoms of the diseases and suggested controls. Some chemical controls are preventive only and won't help once the disease strikes. These fungicides are noted with a (P) in the following section. Other fungicides can be used to control an already established disease and are designated with a (C).

Before buying a fungicide, read the label directions to ensure the product can be used to control the disease in question on your turf.

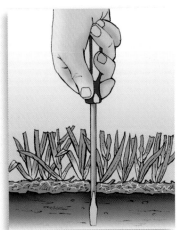

Use a screwdriver to check soil compaction and dryness.

of diseases, water the lawn only when necessary, and then water deeply and thoroughly. When you test your soil with a screwdriver, realize that resistance often adds up to fairly dry soil. If it's quite difficult to force a screwdriver into your soil, it almost certainly needs a good deep watering.

SHADE: When growing in deep shade, grass plants can't manufacture enough chlorophyll. Consequently, the plants grow thin and spindly and are subject to disease. In this situation, replace the struggling grass with a species that is adapted to shade, such as fine fescue, or with a ground cover, such as vinca.

WRONG GRASS: A species that's growing vigorously will not face as many disease pressures as a grass that's struggling. Still, when conditions are right disease can strike. The solution—use disease-resistant varieties. There are hundreds of disease-resistant turfgrass varieties on the market. If your lawn suffers constantly with diseases, try reseeding with a new, disease-resistant variety. Check with your local extension office to learn which diseases are most prevalent in your area and which varieties fare best against them.

POOR SOIL: Compacted soils are a contributing factor to disease because they restrict the growth of roots, which weakens grass plants. Correct compaction by aerating the soil and then topdressing with topsoil and compost.

Even if your soil is in relatively good shape, university studies have shown that topdressing with compost helps to suppress turfgrass diseases.

IDENTIFY THE PROBLEM: If diseases do strike, you can deal with them individually once you are able to recognize their signs.

DISEASE DETECTIVE

Diagnosing a particular disease is a difficult job because many diseases have similar symptoms. And as a disease develops over time, these symptoms may change. However, there are some general clues that can help you to make the call. For best results, you'll need to look closely at individual plants and at the lawn as a whole.

PLANT SYMPTOMS	CAUSE
FUNGAL GROWTH ON THE BLADE	
Long black streaks of powdery spores	Stripe smut
Powdery white dust	Powdery mildew
Red or orange powder	Rust
Gray fungus that is easily rubbed off	Slime mold
SPOTS ON LEAVES BUT NO FUNGUS VISIBLE	
Reddish brown to blue-black, circular or oval	Leaf spot
Straw-colored bands with a reddish brown border	Dollar spot

LAWN SYMPTOMS	CAUSE
CIRCULAR DISEASED AREA	
Present in late winter or early spring	Snow mold
Present in summer, spring, or fall (1 inch to 4 feet or more in diameter)	
Mushrooms present	Fairy ring
No mushrooms	Brown patch
Present in summer, spring, or fall (1 to 8 inches in diameter)	
Throughout the lawn	Dollar spot
Only in full sun, showing green center	Fusarium blight
In low areas and often in streaks	Pythium blight
IRREGULARLY SHAPED DISEASED AREA	
New lawn seedlings wilt and die	Damping-off
Mature lawn affected, spots on leaves	Leaf spot

DISEASES
continued

Brown patch forms large brown to gray spots with wet-looking edges.

Brown Patch

SEASON: Mid- to late summer.
APPEARANCE: Large, irregular circular areas, up to several feet in diameter, occur throughout the lawn. The patches usually have a brownish to gray discoloration with a water-soaked appearance around the edges. Normally, only the leaves and stems are attacked.
FAVORABLE CONDITIONS: High temperatures (75° to 95° F), heavy or dense thatch, high humidity, lush or weak growth from overfertilizing, and excessive moisture create perfect conditions for this disease to thrive in.

SUSCEPTIBLE GRASSES: Serious disease in the South on centipede-grass and St. Augustinegrass. It also attacks bentgrass, bermudagrass, ryegrass, fescue, and zoysiagrass.
RESISTANT VARIETIES: 'Manhattan II', and 'Pennant' perennial ryegrasses; 'Rebel II' and 'Wrangler' tall fescues.
CULTURAL CONTROL: Avoid excessive doses of nitrogen fertilizer, reduce shade and thatch, water deeply when necessary, and keep the lawn aerated.
CHEMICAL CONTROL: Chlorothalonil (P), iprodione (P/C), thiram (P/C), triademefon (P/C) thiophanate-methyl (P/C).

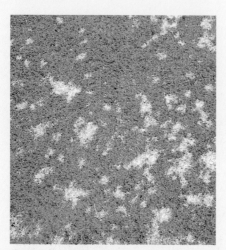

Dollar spot develops numerous small brown patches across a lawn.

Dollar Spot

SEASON: Spring to fall.
APPEARANCE: Grass dies off in small spots from 1 to 5 inches in diameter, but the spots may coalesce into large areas. Spots are usually bleached from tan to straw-colored. White, cobwebby fungus threads may be seen in early morning.
FAVORABLE CONDITIONS: Moderate temperatures, excess moisture, and heavy thatch all contribute to this disease; it is common near foggy coasts. Nitrogen-deficient lawns develop more dollar spot than those that are fertilized adequately.

SUSCEPTIBLE GRASSES: Most severe in bentgrass and bermuda-grass, but also attacks Kentucky bluegrass, fescue, and ryegrass.
RESISTANT VARIETIES: 'Eclipse', 'Adelphi', and 'Midnight' Kentucky bluegrass, 'Biljart' and 'Scaldis' fine fescue; 'Manhattan II' perennial rye.
CULTURAL CONTROL: Increase nitrogen; keep thatch to a minimum; water deeply when necessary, but refrain from watering at night because the water will not evaporate as well as during the day.
CHEMICAL CONTROL: Chlorothalonil (P), iprodione (P/C), thiram (P/C), triademefon (P/C), thiophanate-methyl (P/C).

Fairy ring appears as a circle of dark green grass around a lighter patch.

Fairy Ring

SEASON: Spring to fall.
APPEARANCE: This fungus appears as rings of dark green grass, surrounding areas of dead or light-colored grass. The rings can be produced by the growth of any one of more than 50 kinds of fungus. Grass inside the ring dies because water cannot penetrate the cobwebby surface of the fungus, which lies near the top of the soil. After prolonged wet weather, mushrooms (the fruiting bodies of the fungus) may appear around the edge of the ring, where the fungus is actually growing.

FAVORABLE CONDITIONS: Fairy rings usually develop in soils that contain undecomposed, woody organic matter, such as dead tree roots or old construction materials, such as discarded wood scraps.
SUSCEPTIBLE GRASSES: All.
RESISTANT VARIETIES: None.
CULTURAL CONTROL: Keep the lawn growing by applying adequate nitrogen fertilizer. Try to aerate the ring to improve water penetration. Keep areas wet for two weeks at a time, and make sure you mow frequently.
CHEMICAL CONTROL: Quartenary ammonium compound (P).

Fusarium Patch (Pink snow mold)

SEASON: Fall to spring.
APPEARANCE: Circular patches, 1 to 8 inches in diameter; tiny white or pink masses are sometimes seen on dead leaves. Fungal threads, also white or pink, become visible in early morning. Blades of grass are light tan and stick together. Small, white, or pinkish gel-like spore masses are occasionally seen on dead leaves. This disease is called pink snow mold if it develops under snow or at the margins of melting snowbanks.

FAVORABLE CONDITIONS: Cool temperatures (40° to 60° F) and moisture.
SUSCEPTIBLE GRASSES: Ryegrass, fescue, zoysiagrass, colonial and creeping bentgrasses.
RESISTANT VARIETIES: 'Medallion' and 'Scaldis' fine fescues, 'Eclipse' and 'America' Kentucky bluegrasses, 'Manhattan II' and 'Pennant' perennial ryegrasses.
CULTURAL CONTROL: Reduce shade, improve soil aeration and drainage, avoid excessive nitrogen fertilization in the fall.
CHEMICAL CONTROL: Iprodione (P/C), thiram (P/C), triademefon (P).

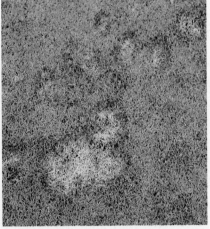

Fusarium patch appears in spring or fall as circles of dead grass.

Leaf Spot

SEASON: Spring to fall.
APPEARANCE: The most obvious symptom of this disease is elongated circular spots on the grass blades. These spots have a brown or straw-colored center with black to purplish borders.
FAVORABLE CONDITIONS: Cool (50° to 70° F), moist conditions are most favorable for the growth of leaf spot. The spots first appear on grass in shady areas of the lawn. They occur most commonly during wet, humid weather or in lawns that are often lightly sprinkled or mowed too closely.

SUSCEPTIBLE GRASSES: Kentucky bluegrass, fescue, and bermudagrass.
RESISTANT VARIETIES: 'Julia' and 'Midnight' Kentucky bluegrasses, 'Banner II' fine fescue, 'Cimarron' and 'Rebel II' tall fescues.
CULTURAL CONTROL: Reduce the amount of shade. Also, improve aeration and drainage and mow at the correct height.
CHEMICAL CONTROL: Chlorothalonil (P), thiophanate-methyl (P).

Leaf spot shows up as small brown circles on grass blades.

Necrotic Ring Spot

SEASON: Spring to fall.
APPEARANCE: "Frog-eye" patterns occur in the lawn; these are small circles of dead grass with a tuft of green grass surrounding and enclosing them. Infected leaves turn reddish purple.
FAVORABLE CONDITIONS: This fungus is the most active at relatively low temperatures (58° to 82° F), but dead spots may not become apparent until warm, dry periods in summer, when they seem to suddenly appear.

SUSCEPTIBLE GRASSES: The most susceptible is Kentucky bluegrass, particularly 'Arboretum', 'Fylking', 'Park', and 'Pennstar'. Bentgrass, creeping bentgrass, and fine fescues can also be attacked.
RESISTANT VARIETIES: None have been identified.
CULTURAL CONTROL: Aerate to improve root growth. Follow correct mowing and watering practices for your grass and conditions. Light, frequent watering helps during drought.
CHEMICAL CONTROL: Iprodione (P), thiophanate-methyl (P/C). Fungicides, along with treatments of nitrogen, can check disease growth.

Necrotic ring spot makes itself known with circular frog-eyes.

DISEASES
continued

One symptom of powdery mildew is a dusty coating on blades.

Powdery Mildew

SEASON: Early summer to fall.
APPEARANCE: First symptoms are light patches of dusty, white to light gray growth on grass blades, especially during cool, rainy weather. Lowest leaves may become completely covered. Although generally not too serious a problem, it can become severe if not controlled. Heavily afflicted areas look as though they've been covered with lime or flour, or sprayed with a coat of white paint.
FAVORABLE CONDITIONS: Slow or non-existent air circulation, shade, and high humidity with temperatures of 60° to 70° F.
SUSCEPTIBLE GRASSES: Kentucky bluegrass, zoysiagrass, and bermudagrass. Lawns growing rapidly because of excessive use of nitrogen fertilizer are extremely susceptible.
RESISTANT VARIETIES: 'Cindy' and 'Flyer' red fescues, 'America' and 'Chateau' Kentucky bluegrasses.
CULTURAL CONTROL: Reduce shade and improve air circulation, be sure to avoid overwatering and overfertilizing.
CHEMICAL CONTROL: Iprodione (P/C), Triademefon (P/C).

Pythium blight appears as patches of soft and slimy grass.

Pythium Blight

SEASON: Summer.
APPEARANCE: The first indication of this disease is the occurrence of irregular patches a few inches in diameter. In those areas, the grass blades appear water-soaked, soft and slimy. The blades soon wither and fade to light brown or straw color, sometimes reddish brown, particularly if the weather is sunny and windy. Then the patches join to form large damaged areas, often several feet in diameter. In the early morning, a white, cottony fungus can be seen on the blades of diseased plants.
FAVORABLE CONDITIONS: High temperatures and excess moisture.
SUSCEPTIBLE GRASSES: Tall fescue, bentgrass, bermudagrass, Kentucky bluegrass, annual ryegrass.
RESISTANT VARIETIES: 'Amigo' tall fescue.
CULTURAL CONTROL: Avoid overwatering, especially newly seeded areas. Make sure the lawn has good drainage. Do not sow turfgrass seed more thickly than recommended. Water established lawns in morning; avoid mowing wet grass in hot weather.
CHEMICAL CONTROL: Chloroneb (P/C), etridiazole (P/C).

Red thread shows up as red or pink strands of fungus on grass blades.

Red Thread

SEASON: Fall.
APPEARANCE: Small spots that appear water-soaked enlarge rapidly to cover a large part of the leaf. As the spots dry, the leaves fade to a light brown or tan. Pink webs bind the grass blades together. Later, the fungus forms thin, red-to-pink, finger-like structures at the tips of grass leaves, which gives the lawn a reddish cast.
FAVORABLE CONDITIONS: Most damaging in spring and fall in temperatures of 68° to 75° F and high humidity. Low levels of nitrogen favor its development. When grass growth slows down due to a lack of nitrogen, the disease then becomes more prevalent.
SUSCEPTIBLE GRASSES: Red fescue, ryegrass, Kentucky bluegrass, and bentgrass.
RESISTANT VARIETIES: 'Biljart' and 'Claudia' fine fescues; 'Chateau' Kentucky bluegrass; 'Pennant' perennial ryegrass.
CULTURAL CONTROL: Maintain an adequate nitrogen level and a soil pH of 6.5 to 7.0; water deeply in the morning.
CHEMICAL CONTROL: Chlorothalonil (P), iprodione (P), triademefon (P/C), thiophanate-methyl (P/C).

Rust

SEASON: Midsummer to fall.
APPEARANCE: The lawn takes on a rust-colored cast, especially noticeable from a distance. Dust-like spores, the main symptom of this disease, form in circular or elongated groups on grass blades. Anything moving through a severely infested area will be covered by the spores, and may spread the disease.
FAVORABLE CONDITIONS: Moderately warm, moist weather. Dew that lasts for 10 to 12 hours promotes germination. Stress that restricts growth favors rust.

SUSCEPTIBLE GRASSES: Can affect most types of turfgrass, but Kentucky bluegrass is damaged most frequently.
RESISTANT VARIETIES: 'America' and 'Eclipse' Kentucky bluegrass, and 'Manhattan II' perennial ryegrass.
CULTURAL CONTROL: Keep the lawn growing rapidly by proper fertilizing with nitrogen and proper watering. This forces the grass to grow upward so it can be mowed off more readily. Mow frequently, every four to five days.
CHEMICAL CONTROL: Chlorothalonil (P), triademefon (P/C).

Rust occurs as reddish pustules or dust on the surface of grass blades.

Stripe Smut

SEASON: Spring to fall.
APPEARANCE: Infected grass plants are usually pale green and stunted. Stripes or streaks made up of spore masses form along the surface of the grass blades, turning from light to dark. Leaves that are affected by stripe smut curl, die, and become shredded by the advancing disease. Affected plants can occur singly or in spots ranging in size from a few inches to more than a foot in diameter. These affected areas will grow more slowly and are generally shorter than surrounding healthy grass.

FAVORABLE CONDITIONS: The moderate temperatures of spring and fall encourage stripe smut. Hot and dry weather will often alleviate or control it.
SUSCEPTIBLE GRASSES: Some varieties of Kentucky bluegrass as well as bentgrass.
RESISTANT VARIETIES: 'America', 'Eclipse', and 'Midnight' Kentucky bluegrasses.
CULTURAL CONTROL: Keep thatch to a minimum, reduce fertilizer applications, and avoid overwatering.
CHEMICAL CONTROL: Tri-ademefon (P), thiophanate-methyl (P/C); best applied in late fall.

Dusty-black stripe smut stunts plants, which turn pale green.

Summer Patch

SEASON: Midsummer.
APPEARANCE: Begins as scattered light green patches up to 8 inches in diameter that turn dull tan to reddish brown. In larger diseased patches, the easiest symptom to recognize is the "frog-eye" pattern— an apparently healthy green patch of grass that is partially or completely surrounded by a ring of dead grass.
FAVORABLE CONDITIONS: Hot, dry, and windy weather creates an excellent climate for summer patch. It's most prevalent when hot (89° to 95° F), sunny days follow warm

periods that have alternated between wet and dry weather.
SUSCEPTIBLE GRASSES: Bentgrass, turf-type tall fescue, perennial ryegrass, and some Kentucky bluegrass cultivars.
RESISTANT VARIETIES: 'America' and 'Blue Star' Kentucky bluegrasses.
CULTURAL CONTROL: Aerate to improve root growth; fertilize with nitrogen, but do not use too much; mow and water correctly. Light, frequent watering helps keep summer patch under control during times of drought.
CHEMICAL CONTROL: Triademe-fon (P), thiophanate-methyl (P/C).

Summer patch develops light green patches up to 8 inches wide.

ENVIRONMENTAL PROBLEMS

Fertilizer spill

CHEMICAL BURNS: Many lawns are damaged by spilled fertilizer, herbicides, gasoline, or by dog urine. These chemical burns are characterized by distinct patches of dead grass. Bright green grass surrounding the patch is typical of burns from fertilizer and dog urine. Both are caused by an abundance of nitrogen.

There are a few ways to remedy chemical burns; you should act quickly and before symptoms appear. For water-soluble material, such as most herbicides, fertilizers, and urine, thoroughly drench the soil with water. For burns caused by insoluble material, such as gasoline or oil, first drench the soil with soapy water, then water thoroughly.

Once the symptoms appear, it is too late to save the browned grass. However, if the

Dry spots

W eeds, insects, diseases—what else could go wrong on the lawn? Believe it or not, there are a few other common problems—chemical burns, low spots with poor drainage, dry spots, scalping, and root competition. Their symptoms often cause them to be mistaken for insect or disease infestations. The following descriptions and prescriptions will help keep you from becoming confused.

Poor drainage

burned area is small, surrounding grass may eventually fill in. If the area doesn't fill in, replace the soil under the dead spots and patch the damaged areas.

LOW SPOTS WITH POOR DRAINAGE: If your lawn has depressions with pale, thinning, weedy turf where standing water gathers, then you have a grading problem that must be corrected. If the low spot is not deep, you can fill it in gradually by spreading small amounts of soil or sand over the low area, allowing the grass to grow up through it. If the drainage problem is more widespread or severe, first try to alleviate it by deeply aerating the wet patch. This should allow water to penetrate farther down into the soil. When the water has drained, roll back the sod, fill in beneath it with topsoil, and replace the turf.

DRY SPOTS: When grasses turn from bright to dull green and lose their luster in patches, the cause could be dry spots. These are often caused by compacted soil, fast draining areas in an otherwise slow-draining lawn, or even buried construction debris. If the blades do not spring back after you walk across them, dryness is the problem. In lawns of cool-season grasses, raise the mower blade about ½ inch when you mow, and make sure to irrigate those areas thoroughly. If compaction is causing the problem, aerate the soil.

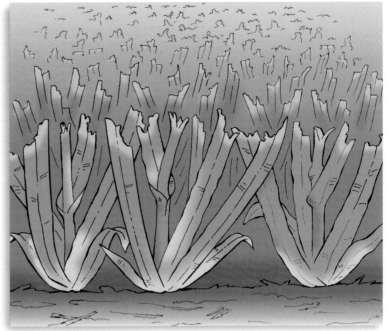

Dull mower blade

Muffler burn

SCALPING OR DULL MOWER INJURY:
If the lawn turns brown soon after mowing, that means you've scalped it—removed too much of the grass blade at one time. It will recover, but raise the height of your mower bed and never cut off more than one-third of the grass blade. If your lawn turns grayish after mowing, you have dull blades. Again, the grass will recover, but be sure to sharpen the blades. Muffler burn occurs when you leave the mower running in one place for a while. It makes an ugly burn, but the spot will heal.

ROOT COMPETITION: Thinning grass that fails to grow vigorously and is more pale than the surrounding lawn may be due to competition from tree roots. To remedy this, give the soil under large trees an extra-deep soaking (from 2 to 6 feet deep, depending on the size and type of tree) two or three times a year. A root waterer (a yard-long hollow probe that channels liquids into the soil from a hose) can also be used to get nutrients down below the roots of the trees. In a shady environment, it is usually best to plant a shade-tolerant grass or ground cover.

Root competition

INDEX

Page numbers followed by t indicate material in tables; numbers in italics denote photographs only.

METRIC CONVERSIONS

U.S. Units to Metric Equivalents			Metric Units to U.S. Equivalents		
To Convert From	Multiply By	To Get	To Convert From	Multiply By	To Get
Inches	25.4	Millimeters	Millimeters	0.0394	Inches
Inches	2.54	Centimeters	Centimeters	0.3937	Inches
Feet	30.48	Centimeters	Centimeters	0.0328	Feet
Feet	0.3048	Meters	Meters	3.2808	Feet
Yards	0.9144	Meters	Meters	1.0936	Yards
Square inches	6.4516	Square centimeters	Square centimeters	0.1550	Square inches
Square feet	0.0929	Square meters	Square meters	10.764	Square feet
Square yards	0.8361	Square meters	Square meters	1.1960	Square yards
Acres	0.4047	Hectares	Hectares	2.4711	Acres
Cubic inches	16.387	Cubic centimeters	Cubic centimeters	0.0610	Cubic inches
Cubic feet	0.0283	Cubic meters	Cubic meters	35.315	Cubic feet
Cubic feet	28.316	Liters	Liters	0.0353	Cubic feet
Cubic yards	0.7646	Cubic meters	Cubic meters	1.308	Cubic yards
Cubic yards	764.55	Liters	Liters	0.0013	Cubic yards

To convert from degrees Fahrenheit (F) to degrees Celsius (C), first subtract 32, then multiply by 5/9.

To convert from degrees Celsius to degrees Fahrenheit, multiply by 9/5, then add 32.